Defense Lawyers

CRIME, JUSTICE, AND PUNISHMENT

Defense Lawyers

Daniel E. Harmon

Austin Sarat, GENERAL EDITOR

CHELSEA HOUSE PUBLISHERS
Philadelphia

Frontispiece: *Defense lawyer Barry Scheck
makes a point as an expert witness looks on.*

Chelsea House Publishers

Editor in Chief Sally Cheney
Director of Production Kim Shinners
Production Manager Pamela Loos
Art Director Sara Davis
Senior Editor John Ziff
Production Editor Diann Grasse
Cover Design Keith Trego

Layout by 21st Century Publishing and
Communications, Inc., New York, N.Y.

First Printing

1 3 5 7 9 8 6 4 2

The Chelsea House World Wide Web address is
http://www.chelseahouse.com

Library of Congress Cataloging-in-Publication Data

Harmon, Daniel E.
Defense lawyers / Daniel E. Harmon
   p. cm. — (Crime, justice, and punishment)
Includes bibliographical references and index.

ISBN 0-7910-4284-7 (alk. paper)

1. Defense (Criminal procedure)—United States—
Juvenile literature. 2. Lawyers—United States—
Juvenile literature. [1. Defense (Criminal procedure)
2. Lawyers.] I. Title II. Series.

KF9619.Z9 H37 2001
345.73'05044—dc21
                                    00-04749

Contents

CRIME, JUSTICE, AND PUNISHMENT

Fears and Fascinations:

An Introduction to
Crime, Justice, and Punishment

By Austin Sarat

We live with crime and images of crime all around us. Crime evokes in most of us a deep aversion, a feeling of profound vulnerability, but it also evokes an equally deep fascination. Today, in major American cities the fear of crime is a major fact of life, some would say a disproportionate response to the realities of crime. Yet the fear of crime is real, palpable in the quickened steps and furtive glances of people walking down darkened streets. At the same time, we eagerly follow crime stories on television and in movies. We watch with a "who done it" curiosity, eager to see the illicit deed done, the investigation undertaken, the miscreant brought to justice and given his just deserts. On the streets the presence of crime is a reminder of our own vulnerability and the precariousness of our taken-for-granted rights and freedoms. On television and in the movies the crime story gives us a chance to probe our own darker motives, to ask "Is there a criminal within?" as well as to feel the collective satisfaction of seeing justice done.

Fear and fascination, these two poles of our engagement with crime, are, of course, only part of the story. Crime is, after all, a major social and legal problem, not just an issue of our individual psychology. Politicians today use our fear of, and fascination with, crime for political advantage. How we respond to crime, as well as to the political uses of the crime issue, tells us a lot about who we are as a people as well as what we value and what we tolerate. Is our response compassionate or severe? Do we seek to understand or to punish, to enact an angry vengeance or to rehabilitate and welcome the criminal back into our midst? The CRIME, JUSTICE, AND PUNISHMENT series is designed to explore these themes, to ask why we are fearful and fascinated, to probe the meanings and motivations of crimes and criminals and of our responses to them, and, finally, to ask what we can learn about ourselves and the society in which we live by examining our responses to crime.

Crime is always a challenge to the prevailing normative order and a test of the values and commitments of law-abiding people. It is sometimes a Raskolnikov-like act of defiance, an assertion of the unwillingness of some to live according to the rules of conduct laid out by organized society. In this sense, crime marks the limits of the law and reminds us of law's all-too-regular failures. Yet sometimes there is more desperation than defiance in criminal acts; sometimes they signal a deep pathology or need in the criminal. To confront crime is thus also to come face-to-face with the reality of social difference, of class privilege and extreme deprivation, of race and racism, of children neglected, abandoned, or abused whose response is to enact on others what they have experienced themselves. And occasionally crime, or what is labeled a criminal act, represents a call for justice, an appeal to a higher moral order against the inadequacies of existing law.

Figuring out the meaning of crime and the motivations of criminals and whether crime arises from defiance, desperation, or the appeal for justice is never an easy task. The motivations and meanings of crime are as varied as are the persons who engage in criminal conduct. They are as mysterious as any of the mysteries of the human soul. Yet the desire to know the secrets of crime and the criminal is a strong one, for in that knowledge may lie one step on the road to protection, if not an assurance of one's own personal safety. Nonetheless, as strong as that desire may be, there is no available technology that can allow us to know the whys of crime with much confidence, let alone a scientific certainty. We can, however, capture something about crime by studying the defiance, desperation, and quest for justice that may be associated with it. Books in the CRIME, JUSTICE, AND PUNISHMENT series will take up that challenge. They tell stories of crime and criminals, some famous, most not, some glamorous and exciting, most mundane and commonplace.

This series will, in addition, take a sober look at American criminal justice, at the procedures through which we investigate crimes and identify criminals, at the institutions in which innocence or guilt is determined. In these procedures and institutions we confront the thrill of the chase as well as the challenge of protecting the rights of those who defy our laws. It is through the efficiency and dedication of law enforcement that we might capture the criminal; it is in the rare instances of their corruption or brutality that we feel perhaps our deepest betrayal. Police, prosecutors, defense lawyers, judges, and jurors administer criminal justice and in their daily actions give substance to the guarantees of the Bill of Rights. What is an adversarial system of justice? How does it work? Why do we have it? Books in the CRIME, JUSTICE, AND PUNISHMENT series will examine the thrill of the chase as we seek to capture the criminal. They will also reveal the drama and majesty of the criminal trial as well as the day-to-day reality of a criminal justice system in which trials are the exception and negotiated pleas of guilty are the rule.

When the trial is over or the plea has been entered, when we have separated the innocent from the guilty, the moment of punishment has arrived. The injunction to punish the guilty, to respond to pain inflicted by inflicting pain, is as old as civilization itself. "An eye for an eye and a tooth for a tooth" is a biblical reminder that punishment must measure pain for pain. But our response to the criminal must be better than and different from the crime itself. The biblical admonition, along with the constitutional prohibition of "cruel and unusual punishment," signals that we seek to punish justly and to be just not only in the determination of who can and should be punished, but in how we punish as well. But neither reminder tells us what to do with the wrongdoer. Do we rape the rapist, or burn the home of the arsonist? Surely justice and decency say no. But, if not, then how can and should we punish? In a world in which punishment is neither identical to the crime nor an automatic response to it, choices must be made and we must make them. Books in the CRIME, JUSTICE, AND PUNISHMENT series will examine those choices and the practices, and politics, of punishment. How do we punish and why do we punish as we do? What can we learn about the rationality and appropriateness of today's responses to crime by examining our past and its responses? What works? Is there, and can there be, a just measure of pain?

CRIME, JUSTICE, AND PUNISHMENT brings together books on some of the great themes of human social life. The books in this series capture our fear and fascination with crime and examine our responses to it. They remind us of the deadly seriousness of these subjects. They bring together themes in law, literature, and popular culture to challenge us to think again, to think anew, about subjects that go to the heart of who we are and how we can and will live together.

*   *   *   *   *

From Abraham Lincoln to Johnnie Cochran, from Clarence Darrow to F. Lee Bailey, there are perhaps no more important or storied figures in the criminal justice system than defense lawyers. Alternatively portrayed as heroic defenders of individual rights and crusaders for justice against the over whelming power of the state, those lawyers sometimes assume almost mythic proportions. Yet other images cast defense lawyers in a different light. In these other images defense lawyers are depicted as cynically selling out their clients, manipulating unsophisticated people into pleading guilty, and cooperating with prosecutors to railroad the innocent. Can both of these images be true? Readers can turn to *Defense Lawyers* to shed light on these and other images of those whose job it is to stand up to the state.

This book provides a vivid portrait of the wide-ranging types of criminal defense lawyers. So varied and complex are the roles these lawyers play that it is hard to identify what they have in common beyond their work in the face of accusation. The tasks and challenges of public defenders are very different from the work of those who specialize in defending white-collar criminals. Combining lively portraits of famous defense lawyers with intriguing examples from actual cases, *Defense Lawyers* will be an invaluable resource for those seeking to understand one of the crucial factors in our adversarial system of justice.

THE DEFENSE

Judd Gray was a hapless salesman enticed by an attractive woman to do anything she asked—murder included. At least, that was the argument his lawyer made when Gray was tried in New York in 1927, along with his lover, Ruth Snyder. The charge against them: killing Albert Snyder, Ruth's husband, with a sash weight.

The two, whose trial engrossed the nation, were clearly guilty. The only real question: was one of them *less* guilty than the other, and therefore deserving of leniency? Gray's defense lawyer described Ruth Snyder as a "poisonous snake" who made a slave of Gray. Snyder's lawyer countered by casting all the blame on the salesman.

This desperate legal strategy failed for both defendants. Convicted, they were executed at Sing Sing Prison the following year. Ruth Snyder went down in history with a macabre distinction: she was the first prisoner to be photographed (against prison

Ruth Snyder and her lawyers listen to testimony during the sensational 1927 murder trial of Snyder and her lover, Judd Gray. Each defendant tried unsuccessfully to blame the other for killing Snyder's husband, Albert. Both eventually received the death penalty.

regulations) while dying in the electric chair.

Thirty years later, a young New Mexico man named José Franco Padilla was tried for kidnapping a five-year-old girl, raping her, and stabbing her to death with a screwdriver. He confessed and was convicted.

End of case? No. The defendant's lawyer had asked the judge to deal with a legal concept called "diminished capacity" while instructing the jury. Although not legally insane, Padilla, the lawyer maintained, was under a "defect of the mind" when he committed the atrocity, and therefore didn't really know what he was doing. It seemed plausible, since Padilla had apparently been drinking beer and smoking marijuana for 12 hours before abducting the child. If the diminished capacity consideration was permitted, the jury could find Padilla guilty of a lesser degree of murder, which could dramatically affect the sentence.

The trial judge rejected the request. But later the state supreme court overturned the first-degree murder conviction, ruling that diminished capacity should have been explained to the jury as a possible factor in the case.

News media heavily cover dramatic cases like these. They often report the details far outside the jurisdictions in which the events take place—sometimes nationwide and abroad. Courtroom contests like those of Padilla or Gray and Snyder pale in the public eye, though, when compared with the so-called trial of the century. That 1995 event got its label even before it began. From the moment it was first reported, the gory murder of Nicole Brown Simpson and her friend Ronald L. Goldman riveted America's attention to Los Angeles. And when Nicole's famous ex-husband, former professional football star O. J. Simpson, was named the prime suspect and denied any involvement, the "trial of the century" label was assured.

Simpson's criminal trial (which was followed by a civil trial) had the kind of ingredients American audiences seem to want: a celebrity, a stormy marriage, a ghastly knife slaying. It opened a Pandora's box of legal issues, ranging from alleged false testimony and evidence-tampering to the reliability of scientific evidence to accusations of racial prejudice on all sides. The Simpson criminal trial was of special interest to those studying the techniques and art of trial defense. Simpson retained a "dream team" of savvy lawyers known for representing famous people, and they were assisted by other noted lawyers, investigators, and medical specialists.

The Simpson criminal trial was not a landmark case in terms of judicial significance. But of all recent trials—both the pivotally important and the merely spectacular—it is probably the one that will be best remembered. As a showcase for legal defense styles, strategies, and tactics, it was an open classroom.

When the trial was finally over—after more than eight months of motions, testimony, and arguments, much of which were nationally televised—it left a nation divided. Simpson's acquittal prompted outraged protests from millions who believed a vicious murderer had been set free, along with cheers of joy from others who believed he could never have committed such an act.

Three sensational cases. Three different defense strategies. In one, lawyers unsuccessfully played codefendants against each other. In another, an advocate hammered on a point of law to win clemency for his client. In the last, one of the most potent teams of defense lawyers and support staff in history employed a varied arsenal of strategies, tactics, and techniques, leaving behind a morass of legal and ethical questions, some of them to be debated for generations to come.

Criminal defense is an area of law practice that

Members of O. J. Simpson's legal "dream team" huddle during Simpson's murder trial. From left: Alan Dershowitz, Johnnie Cochran, Robert Shapiro. The defendant is at right.

has special demands. Many lawyers devote all or most of their career to criminal defense cases. For a criminal defense lawyer, each new case presents a challenge. Many matters are basically redundant—endless drug busts under similar circumstances, for example, do not often warrant unique legal strategies or result in surprise acquittals or sentences. Other cases are remarkable and fascinating, with features that must be probed carefully. Regardless of the straightforward or complex nature of each case, an individual's rights and future are at stake. It is the duty of the defense lawyer to vigorously defend that individual and ensure that his or her rights are upheld.

This book will examine the defense lawyer's profession. By discussing some of the notable defenders throughout the nation's history, it will show what these professionals try to accomplish, the ethical tensions they struggle to balance, and changes that have affected not just their work, but also the overall American system of justice.

THE
DEFENDER'S
ROLE

criminal law makes for great story lines in American popular literature and screen productions: A hapless defendant, wrongly accused of some appalling crime, is on the brink of ruin. He faces a long prison term, loss of family, job, reputation—even, perhaps, execution. A diligent lawyer takes the case, but the facts seem indisputable, and they all line up against the accused. Everyone is convinced of the defendant's guilt.

Our hero, the defense attorney, cannot find so much as a rough pebble on which to begin constructing a defense . . . until an offhand, unrelated comment by a friend at a lunch counter switches on the mental light-bulb. Suddenly the evidence is cast in an entirely new light, and the shadow of guilt falls not on the poor client, but on a character *no one* would ever have suspected. We rejoice with the exonerated client and marvel at the lawyer's ability to pull a rabbit from a hat. Meanwhile, we realize that our criminal justice system, though

A wavering witness and a defense lawyer getting ready to bore in: Hollywood's view of the typical trial. In reality, much of the work of defense lawyers is routine. The vast majority of cases are settled through plea bargaining.

19

caught momentarily on the ropes, still works.

In real life, defense lawyers don't get to be Hollywood-style heroes very often. Actually, they are viewed warily by much of the American public. We often think of them as wily manipulators who are paid—and generally paid well—to get bad people off the hook. "The truth is that most criminal defendants are, in fact, guilty," acknowledged the noted defense lawyer and law professor Alan M. Dershowitz in his book *Reasonable Doubts*. Most commentators on criminal justice agree.

So there are grounds for the public's cynicism. But defense lawyers also have a job to do—a job mandated by the Constitution of the United States and minutely defined by two centuries of court rulings. Legal defendants cannot be forced by law to tell the truth about what they did or did not do (although people who testify in court must take an oath pledging to tell the truth). The law does require, however, that all defendants be granted certain rights, regardless of whether they are guilty or innocent and whether they choose to admit wrongdoing. The defense lawyer must work to secure those rights.

Vigorous legal defense is an essential part of our democratic society. True, defense lawyers sometimes help guilty people escape punishment. On the other hand, they sometimes protect innocent people from being punished, and they see that people who admit their guilt are not punished excessively. No judicial system is perfect. Mainstream legal thinking in the United States holds that it is far better to err on the side of innocence, that it is more acceptable for a guilty party to go free than for an innocent party to endure unwarranted punishment.

Much of the defense lawyer's tool kit is based on the Bill of Rights—the first 10 amendments to the Constitution. Among other assurances, the Bill of Rights guarantees that:

- a person's home may not be searched, nor may his or her property be seized by police, unless the authorities have reasonable cause to suspect criminal activity
- a person cannot be tried twice on the same charge (this is referred to as "double jeopardy")
- legal defendants do not have to testify against themselves
- no defendant can be punished or fined until "due process" has been carried out in the appropriate courts
- every criminal defendant may request a trial at which he or she can see accusing witnesses and hear their testimony, and in turn can present defense witnesses
- every defendant is offered legal counsel
- the defendant is not burdened with excessive bail.

Law professor and defense attorney Alan Dershowitz has pointed out that most criminal defendants are guilty. On the other hand, Dershowitz also maintains that police are trained informally to lie.

In the United States, anyone charged with a crime is entitled to representation by a lawyer (a right not guaranteed in every country). If the person cannot afford a lawyer, the court system will appoint one—typically, a public defender—to handle the case. The defendant may ask that the lawyer be present during questioning by police. The defendant is not required to answer any questions or make any statements about the matter under investigation; in fact, police must warn the suspect that any statements might be used as adverse evidence in court. Police are required to explain these rights to suspects immediately upon making an arrest. This requirement is based on a famous 1966 Supreme Court case, *Miranda v. Arizona.*

Among their other duties, criminal defense lawyers must be sure police have obeyed the *Miranda* ruling fully in their clients' cases. They know that in the confusion and stress of an arrest, an innocent person might say things he or she thinks the police want to hear, even though the statements may be incorrect or misleading.

The rights of defendants in America have been debated and formulated over many generations. The underlying concept is that every defendant must be presumed innocent until proven guilty. Time has taught us that even when an individual's guilt or motivations at first seem obvious, certain factors and evidence may eventually come to light to reveal a very different picture of what really happened.

Defense lawyers usually come to public notice through media coverage of criminal trials—the focus of this book. Much defense work, meanwhile, is performed in less sensational civil matters. What's the distinction?

Civil cases are sometimes called private cases because they involve actions by and against private citizens or private businesses. Typically they are cases in which one citizen (the plaintiff) files an accusation, or legal complaint, against another (the defendant). These matters are usually less serious than criminal matters; the defendant, even if proved to be at fault, is not considered a criminal.

For example, the complaint may be brought by a person alleging injuries and/or damage in an automobile accident, claiming the defendant was responsible; by an employee against a company for an injury sustained on the job that was possibly caused by unsafe working conditions; by a customer who claims to have been sickened or injured by a product sold by a certain business or manufacturer; by a resident who claims that part of a neighbor's vegetable garden has been planted on the plaintiff's property, destroying the grass—or perhaps that the neighbor's dog has trespassed and destroyed the plaintiff's own garden. The types of civil cases are almost endless.

Most of these cases never go to trial. After the proper pretrial motions (formal allegations and responses) are filed, the strengths and weaknesses of each side's case are apparent to their lawyers. The lawyers often negotiate a settlement before having to enter a courtroom.

Criminal cases, on the other hand, are thought of as public cases because the general public has an overriding interest in their outcome. A crime such as murder, assault, or robbery is not simply a private matter between the criminal and the victim. Under the law, crime is first and foremost an offense against the social order—against society as a whole. So when legal proceedings are initiated after a criminal suspect's arrest, the case is not titled in court records *Victim A v. Defendant Z*, but *The People v. Defendant Z*. The crime is legally considered to have been committed not against an individual victim, but against society—that is, the people of a state. A public prosecutor (rather than a private plaintiff's lawyer) presents the case for the public and, in a sense, functions as counsel for both the victim and "the people."

It isn't always necessary that a criminal actually *commit* an act against society in order to be prosecuted. An *attempted* crime may also be a legal violation, although it usually brings a lesser punishment than would the crime itself. Criminal attempts, which we will examine more fully later, can be difficult to prove.

Often criminal cases involve violent acts. However, certain types of "paper crimes" (for example, extortion, fraud, and tax evasion) are also criminal acts. Again, the alleged offender is opposed by the state, representing the people, not just one particular victim.

As in civil matters, most criminal cases are resolved out of court. The most famous defense lawyers may be the ones who win sensational cases at trial. The most effective ones, however, are arguably those who rarely appear before a trial jury. They convince the prosecution beforehand that conviction, for a variety of reasons, is unlikely. They may win outright dismissal of the case. If not, they may obtain for their client a plea bargain—an agreement to plead guilty to a lesser charge with less-severe punishment.

The double murder of Nicole Brown Simpson and Ronald Goldman was a rare case in which the defendant (O. J. Simpson) was eventually placed on trial in both criminal and civil courts. Though acquitted of the charge of murder in the criminal trial, he was nonetheless found responsible for wrongful death in the civil trial. A criminal conviction would have called for life imprisonment; the civil conviction resulted in heavy fines.

Naturally, criminal and civil cases are not heard or tried in the same setting. You won't observe a murder trial immediately followed—in the same courtroom, presided over by the same judge—by the trial of a person being sued for lawn mower damages to a neighbor's flower bed. The U.S. judicial system has different types of courts for different types of matters.

Courts are set up at different levels of government. Municipal courts handle actions that may have violated a town or city's unique laws and regulations. Statewide courts (often divided into judicial circuits within the state) adjudicate matters involving state laws. Federal courts hear cases in which federal laws may have been violated.

And there are specialized courts that hear specific types of matters. These range from traffic courts (speeding and other traffic charges) and family courts (divorce settlements, child custody disputes, and so on) to admiralty courts (maritime issues) and bankruptcy courts.

Whatever the setting, a central idea in America's judicial system is the "burden of proof." A defendant is not required by law to prove his or her innocence, and in fact the defense is not required to enter any exculpatory evidence at all. Instead, the plaintiff or prosecutor must prove the defendant's guilt. And, until proven otherwise, a jury must presume that an accused party is innocent. The accuser—prosecutor or plaintiff—bears the burden of proof.

O. J. Simpson talks with his lead attorney, Robert Baker, during a recess in his civil trial for the wrongful deaths of Nicole Brown Simpson and Ronald Goldman. The rules and standards of evidence differ between criminal and civil matters, and many defense lawyers specialize in one type of case.

In most criminal trials, the defense lawyer will remind the jury that the burden of proof rests with the prosecution. In closing arguments, the defender typically argues that the burden of proof has not been met.

In civil cases, the verdict is usually based on the "preponderance of evidence" that has been presented. This means that the fact finder—judge or jury—must simply decide whether most of the evidence has shown that the vital facts in question are probably true or probably false.

Criminal trials involve a more stringent standard. In order for a conviction to result from a criminal charge, the defendant's guilt must be established "beyond a reasonable doubt"—and in most cases the jury must vote unanimously for conviction. One or more dissenting votes results in what is called a hung jury; when this happens, the prosecution has the option of retrying the case. Sometimes, rather than repeat the trial before a different jury, the prosecution will agree to accept a plea of guilty to a lesser charge; or, depending on the gravity of the crime and the prospects for conviction at a second trial, the matter may be dropped altogether.

Key to the criminal defender's work is drawing the distinction between factual guilt and legal guilt. Although the facts of a case may indicate clearly that a client is guilty, the prosecution may falter if the defense can show that law enforcement officers or the court system itself has failed to abide by any of a number of rules of law. Here are a few examples:

- Police searches and seizures must be conducted according to strict legal guidelines.
- Defendants must be granted hearings without "unnecessary delay."
- The specific law that is said to have been broken must actually apply to the circumstances of the crime. We may think this is a ridiculously obvious requirement in a court case, but there are subtle differences in some types of related laws. There are varying

degrees of homicide and certain other crimes, for instance. Which degree precisely applies to the crime under consideration? Questions such as criminal "intent" and "attempt" are often difficult to establish but can have a decisive bearing on the applicable law.

- The defendant has a right to an impartial judge. In appeals, convicted defendants often claim that presiding judges should have excused themselves because of various judicial connections, past records, or statements they made during or outside the trials.

Whatever the outcome of any case, the U.S. system of justice is rooted firmly in the presumption of innocence. The defense lawyer's appointed role is to make sure the defendant is, in fact, presumed innocent until proven guilty.

In the next chapter we will profile some of America's best-known courtroom defenders.

Assistant police chief John Love of Sullivan, Illinois, stands outside a trailer home where a drug arrest he made triggered a search-and-seizure controversy that was eventually sorted out by the Supreme Court. One of the defense lawyer's tasks is to make sure authorities have followed proper procedures in gathering evidence.

FAMOUS DEFENDERS

Abraham Lincoln

"Fair play is a jewel," Abraham Lincoln once wrote. The young, rail-splitting farmer who would rise to lead America through its gravest crisis always championed fairness and equality.

Born in 1809 in Kentucky and raised in the wilds, Lincoln obtained less than a year of formal schooling. But after learning the basics of reading, writing, and arithmetic, he set out to educate himself. He would walk many miles to borrow books—any books he could find. Lincoln especially liked to read and hear stories, and while still in his teens he became popular as a teller of homespun tales at country stores. It was a talent that would serve him well as a lawyer and politician.

Lincoln became so well liked that he was chosen captain of a militia unit during the frontier Indian Wars of the 1830s. In 1834 he was elected to the state

Abraham Lincoln, the future 16th president of the United States, argues a case during his days as a defense attorney in Springfield, Illinois. Lincoln's devotion to ethical conduct in the practice of law won him many admirers.

legislature in Illinois, where he was then living. That same year, he decided to study law. There was no law school for him to attend; he simply read law books borrowed from John Stuart, a lawyer in Springfield, Illinois. Two years later, he received a law license, and in 1837 he joined Stuart's firm as junior partner.

The fledgling attorney represented clients in various courts, from the office of the local justice of the peace all the way up to the Illinois Supreme Court. He traveled for months at a time, following the area judge in a circuit of court sessions throughout 15 counties. The tall, bony lawyer quickly became respected for his ability to explain legal matters to poorly educated jurors, while at the same time impressing judges with his legal wisdom. He won many cases through his story-telling skills, but he was also a careful logician who spent much time preparing his cases. When not advocating before the bench as defense or plaintiff's counsel, he occasionally served as a substitute for the regular circuit judge. In his leisure time, Lincoln was often asked to referee races and cockfights.

Whenever possible, he preferred to help his clients settle matters out of court. Sometimes this meant that he received only a token fee for his time and knowledge of the law. Nevertheless, he was firmly committed to avoiding unnecessary court actions. "Never stir up litigation," he once wrote. "A worse man can scarcely be found than one who does this."

Debt collection cases were common in those years. Lincoln represented both plaintiffs and defendants. His reputation for honesty, combined with his art of simple communication, earned him many clients.

After serving a term in the United States Congress, Lincoln returned to law practice in 1849 and became one of the most prominent lawyers in Illinois. When he successfully defended the Illinois Central Railroad against tax law charges—an early allegation of white-collar crime—he earned a fee of $5,000. This was an enormous sum in the mid-1800s.

The once-poor woodsman had become a prosperous lawyer, but his heart was in greater issues affecting the nation. With his dynamic speeches opposing slavery, he became a national political leader. His law career ended when he took office as president in March 1861; the Civil War began the next month. Lincoln was assassinated four years later, less than a week after the war had ended.

In his writings, Lincoln left behind advice to aspiring lawyers: "If you are resolutely determined to make a lawyer of yourself, the thing is more than half done already. . . . Always bear in mind that your own resolution to succeed, is more important than any other one thing."

Clarence Darrow

The Scopes "Monkey Trial" of 1925 remains one of the best-remembered court cases in American history. It also stands as a landmark in the career of one of America's most famous defense lawyers, Clarence Darrow.

A schoolteacher in Tennessee named John Scopes was charged with teaching evolution, in violation of state law. According to the scientific theory of evolution, all complex organisms, including humans, developed over millions of years from gradual changes that occurred to simpler organisms. Humans' ancestors, the theory states, include apes—hence the popular name of the Scopes trial.

Among conservative Christians, evolution was—and to some extent, still is—controversial because it conflicts with a literal interpretation of the biblical story of creation. In the Bible version, found in the first chapter of Genesis, God creates the world and all its plant and animal species in six days. When the origins of the human race were taught in Tennessee schools, the Genesis creation account was presented.

The Scopes trial drew national news coverage and heated commentary far and wide. Part of the reason was the eloquent argument offered on Scopes's behalf by the aging, celebrated defense lawyer Clarence Darrow. Despite the fact that he officially lost the case, it was to be the crowning moment in a long, dramatic career.

Darrow was born in Kinsman, Ohio, in 1857. In his early twenties, after studying law for a year at the University of Michigan, he began accepting clients in his home state. He then moved to Chicago. By the time he was 40, he'd made a name for himself as a legal defender of labor unions.

His first famous case was in 1894, when he defended labor leaders in a railroad strike that was delaying the U.S. mail. In 1911, he represented two brothers, both union leaders, who were accused of dynamiting a news-paper building in Los Angeles with fatal results. Sur-prisingly, Darrow entered a guilty plea—thus saving his clients from an almost certain death sentence.

This strategy was repeated in 1924, when Darrow agreed to represent murder defendants Nathan Leopold and Richard Loeb in Chicago. Until the Simpson trial of 1995, the Leopold-Loeb case was widely regarded as the "trial of the century" for two reasons. First was the sensational nature of the cold-blooded felony: the two young men, brilliant students who seemed to have out-standing professional careers before them, apparently wanted to see if they could commit the "perfect crime." Second was the fact that, at the urging of the defen-dants' families, the legendary defense lawyer agreed to take their case.

Leopold and Loeb were accused of viciously murder-ing a 14-year-old boy in their well-to-do neighborhood, dumping his mutilated body in a culvert, and phoning his home to demand a ransom. Solid evidence against them mounted, their statements to the police became confused and contradictory, and they soon admitted the deed. Darrow took the case not because he sympathized with them personally, but because he firmly opposed the death penalty.

Clarence Darrow (standing, arms folded) cross-examines William Jennings Bryan during the Scopes "Monkey Trial," July 1925.

By having the defendants plead guilty, Darrow ensured that the sentencing arguments would be heard not by an outraged jury, but by a lone judge. Darrow was able to persuade the judge that executing the two men would not benefit society. Each defendant was sentenced to life in prison plus 99 years. (Loeb was killed in a prison fight a few years later; Leopold served more than 30 years and was released.)

Darrow employed a similar strategy the following year in the Scopes defense. After using the packed courtroom to attack biblical teachings on the origins of human life and to embarrass his longtime rival, orator William Jennings Bryan (whom he sarcastically called to testify as an "expert" on the Bible), Darrow entered a guilty plea. This meant that there would be no closing arguments—the forum in which Bryan had expected to win the evolution debate. Historians generally agree that despite conceding his client's guilt, Darrow won the underlying contest.

Ironically, the trial was staged—"part test case, part publicity stunt," in the words of one chronicler. The state law prohibiting the teaching of evolution was never strictly enforced to begin with; Scopes was a physics teacher, not a biology teacher; he made Darwin's theory part of his students' assigned reading but didn't debate the issue in class; and he agreed to participate in the arrest and trial with the understanding that he could have his teaching job back when it was over. The trial was designed as a media event. Those with vested interests reportedly included local business and municipal leaders, who wanted the publicity; the fledgling American Civil Liberties Union, which wanted an issue of national significance to challenge; and the rival lawyers, vying for popular recognition as America's champion orator.

Many historians and commentators regard Darrow as the most important defense lawyer in U.S. history. He died in 1938.

F. Lee Bailey

In the minds of many Americans, F. Lee Bailey looms as the most famous modern defense lawyer for his representation in sensational, often gory cases. He was one of the lawyers who successfully cleared O. J. Simpson of criminal murder charges in 1995. However, Bailey's had already become a household name by the 1960s, when he succeeded in winning the reversal of a guilty verdict against a wealthy doctor, Sam Sheppard.

A Massachusetts native, Bailey began his legal career in the U.S. Marine Corps, where as a volunteer legal officer he learned to research military cases. Later, while earning his law degree at Boston University, he ran his own detective agency. In one of his first trials as a civilian lawyer, he employed polygraph (lie detection) testing to help win acquittal for a man police called the Torso Murderer, who had allegedly beheaded his wife.

Because of its gruesome nature, that 1960 case made headlines—for Bailey, as well as for the defendant. A year later Bailey was hired to take on the case of Sam Sheppard in Ohio. Sheppard, convicted in a sensational 1954 trial for brutally murdering his pregnant wife, was serving a life sentence.

Sifting through thousands of pages of documents and questioning countless individuals who had been involved in the original trial, Bailey worked on the case for three years. Finally, he was able to show that the trial judge had been prejudiced against the defendant. The judge had been openly hostile toward Sheppard and his counsel in court; this attitude was in keeping with that of the media, which, according to critics, had "tried the case in the press."

Bailey obtained Sheppard's release on bail, then pressed the case all the way to the U.S. Supreme Court, which in 1965 ordered a new trial. In 1966, Bailey defended Sheppard brilliantly in the retrial, discrediting the prosecution's evidence and winning his client's acquittal.

One case Bailey lost—but one that nevertheless added to his national recognition as a highly sought-after defense lawyer—was his defense of Albert DeSalvo, the self-proclaimed "Boston Strangler." Bailey was seeking not acquittal, but a declaration of insanity. The jury at the 1967 trial rejected Bailey's argument; DeSalvo was sentenced to life imprisonment (he was murdered by a fellow inmate six years later).

A departure for Bailey was his defense of U.S. Army captain Ernest Medina in the early 1970s. American soldiers under Medina's command in Vietnam carried out the infamous My Lai Massacre, in which more than 500 unarmed Vietnamese villagers—men, women, and children—were shot to death. Medina and the officer in command of the patrol, Lieutenant William Calley, were court-martialed. Calley's defense was that Medina, his commanding officer, had ordered the slaughter; thus, Calley was merely carrying out a military duty. Bailey countered by presenting witnesses who testified that Medina had not ordered the killing, had been unaware it was happening, and, upon learning of it, had ordered the bloodshed to cease. Calley was found guilty of murder; Medina was acquitted.

Bailey was hired to defend Patricia Hearst, the young heiress to a California newspaper dynasty, in 1976. In February 1974, while a college student, Hearst had been abducted by a militant left-wing group that called itself the Symbionese Liberation Army, or SLA. Within two months the case had taken a bizarre turn: on a tape released by the SLA, Hearst announced that she had joined her captors. Later, she joined SLA members in the armed robbery of a San Francisco bank. The Federal Bureau of Investigation ultimately changed her status from abductee to bank robber. Wanted posters bearing her smiling face began to appear across the country. When she was finally found nearly two years after being abducted, Hearst was placed under arrest.

Bailey's defense was that Hearst had been a virtual prisoner of war throughout her 20-month absence, brainwashed and forced to obey her kidnappers' orders. Some observers believed it was among Bailey's worst courtroom performances, capped by a confusing, ineffective closing argument. Though many expected Hearst to be acquitted, the prosecution convinced the jury she had been in control of her criminal actions. She spent three years in prison before President Jimmy Carter commuted her sentence.

These and other front-page affairs earned Bailey a reputation and lifestyle as a jet-setting celebrity lawyer. He eagerly courted publicity. (He reportedly had high-intensity lights installed in his office for TV crews to use

F. Lee Bailey has earned a reputation for dogged, relentless cross-examination.

at impromptu press conferences.) Bar organizations in Massachusetts and New Jersey imposed sanctions on his practice because of his publicity ploys.

His career suffered more damage: He found himself charged with mail fraud in 1973, and in 1982 he was arrested in California for drunk driving; he succeeded in beating both charges. In 1996, after the Simpson verdict, Bailey spent six weeks in prison for failing to comply with a federal court order while representing an accused drug trafficker.

Bailey's most prominent role as part of Simpson's

defense team was impeaching the credibility of police detective Mark Fuhrman. By depicting Fuhrman as a racist during a three-day cross-examination, Bailey is thought to have turned the jury's attention from the charges at hand to the impression that a white detective had been bent on framing a black defendant.

While representing defendants in some of the most spectacular and emotionally charged trials of the late 20th century, Bailey also wrote or coauthored a number of books.

William Kunstler

His defense of the radical activists called the Chicago Seven sealed William Kunstler's reputation in 1969–70. At the height of the Vietnam War and the civil rights era, Kunstler came to be called Wild Bill, defender of modern-day outlaws.

Born to a wealthy New York family in 1919, Kunstler graduated from Yale University and served as an army intelligence officer in World War II. After establishing a law practice, he became a civil rights activist in 1961, working with the Freedom Riders, who defied arrest to challenge public segregation policies. Racial segregation, though unconstitutional, was practiced widely in the South and to a lesser extent in other parts of America— even in Washington, D.C. In repeated cases, Kunstler defended African-American civil rights activists who were arrested after they demanded service at all-white business establishments. He usually won their quick release.

He also defended peace activists who opposed the Vietnam War. Among his most famous clients were brothers Daniel and Philip Berrigan, Catholic priests who had raided Selective Service System offices in Maryland and damaged and destroyed army draft records. Kunstler and his cocounsel Harrop Freeman lost the 1968 trial; the Berrigans were convicted and sentenced to prison terms. The following year, however, Kunstler was back in the news, arguing what was undoubtedly his most significant case.

The Vietnam War dramatically divided Americans in the late 1960s and early 1970s. Because of it, anti-war radicals targeted the 1968 Democratic National Convention in Chicago as an ideal event at which to confront authorities and to fan the flames of their movement, assured of international media coverage. The Chicago Seven (initially there were eight defendants; one case was separated from the others) were left-wing militants who allegedly conspired to incite rioting at the convention. The riots were well documented on nationwide television—violent confrontations between thousands of war protesters and police.

Americans have become accustomed to the circus atmosphere that marks some courtroom proceedings today. Possibly no trial, however, has been more chaotic than the lengthy Chicago affair. Bobby Seale, one of the defendants, was so boisterous that the judge ordered him, struggling, to be tied to a chair and gagged. Kunstler protested the order as "medieval torture"—although Seale had gone on record rejecting Kunstler and cocounsel Leonard Weinglass as his legal representatives. (The judge soon ordered a mistrial for Seale, removing his case from the proceedings at hand.)

The other defendants were less violent but hardly less contemptuous of the court—part of the government "establishment" they opposed. To their aid, Kunstler summoned a parade of famous character witnesses, including best-selling authors and folk music performers and songwriters. There was little to be done to disprove the charges, however, in the face of overwhelming prosecution evidence. Five of the seven defendants were found guilty of conspiracy to riot. Furthermore, the judge handed down more than 150 contempt-of-court citations—including citations against Kunstler, who was sentenced to four years!

Ironically, a court of appeals eventually overturned the conspiracy convictions as well as the contempt

William Kunstler (right) gets a hug from Chicago Seven defendant Jerry Rubin after a judge overturned contempt-of-court sentences.

citations. Apart from a public mockery of the court and the "establishment" in general, the five-month episode had accomplished little.

It solidified Kunstler's stature, however, not just as a lawyer but as a self-professed "radical." He began earning most of his income from lectures, allowing him to represent many of his dissident clients free of charge. He championed the causes of prison inmates in Attica, New York, who rioted against prison conditions (resulting in 39 deaths), and of Native Americans who staged a siege on a South Dakota reservation and allegedly murdered two FBI agents. Another high-profile case was his defense of Gregory Lee "Joey" Johnson, who burned an American flag as a political protest in 1984. Kunstler successfully argued before the U.S. Supreme Court in 1989 that flag burning was a form of free speech protected by the First Amendment to the Constitution.

Kunstler, who titled his autobiography *My Life as a Radical Lawyer*, voiced opposition to the American system of government throughout his later years. He died of a heart attack in 1995.

Gerry Spence

Some of America's most famous trial lawyers have built their reputations on defending a particular type of client. Gerry Spence, on the other hand, has won cases for individuals and causes notable for their vast differences, and he represents both plaintiffs and defendants.

Spence, a self-proclaimed "country lawyer" from Wyoming, represented the plaintiff in what was probably his most famous case. In 1974 a lab technician named Karen Silkwood informed the government of apparent negligence and mismanagement at the Kerr-McGee nuclear facility in Oklahoma, where she worked. A few months later, Silkwood was killed in a mysterious auto accident. An autopsy, like medical tests she'd had while living, showed the presence of plutonium, a highly radioactive element produced by nuclear reactors, in her body. Representatives of her estate sued Kerr-McGee, claiming that the company's negligence had caused Silkwood's plutonium poisoning.

When the case was tried in 1979, Spence vigorously challenged Kerr-McGee employees and outside experts who claimed that the plutonium level in Silkwood's body was within government guidelines. He cross-examined one key scientific witness for two days, getting the expert to admit among other things that scientists weren't sure how much plutonium exposure might be safe before cancer became a serious risk.

At the end of the two-month trial, the jury awarded more than $10 million in damages to the Silkwood estate. (Seven years later, during the appeals process, the parties agreed to an out-of-court settlement of $1.38 million.)

In 1990, Spence was hired to plead a quite different

case. Imelda Marcos, the extravagant former first lady of the Philippines, faced racketeering charges in the wake of her husband's fall from power. Marcos stood accused of illegally using her influence for personal gain. Typically, Spence has refused to represent celebrity clients or monied interests. But in the Marcos case he made an exception, noting overriding considerations that pointed up the important issue of liberty. After a lengthy trial in New York, Spence won an acquittal for Marcos.

Three years later, Spence championed a very different cause: the case of Randy Weaver, a former Green Beret arrested after a bloody standoff with federal law enforcement agents in Idaho. When officers attempted to apprehend Weaver on gun violation charges, a gunfight broke out near his remote Ruby Ridge cabin. Weaver's son and a deputy U.S. marshal died in the shoot-out. During the succeeding law enforcement siege of the cabin, an FBI sharpshooter killed Weaver's wife.

At the trial, government prosecutors depicted Weaver as a dangerous white supremacist. Spence, however, maintained that Weaver and his family had simply sought to withdraw from society. In cross-examining government witnesses, Spence exposed evidence of an FBI cover-up of certain details of the confrontation at Ruby Ridge. Then, in a brilliant defensive tactic, he rested his case without calling any witnesses for his client—suggesting that he considered the prosecution's case so weak no defense was necessary.

Spence won not-guilty verdicts on charges of murder, assault, conspiracy, and firearms violations. Weaver later filed a civil lawsuit against the government and won $3.1 million in damages for the loss of his wife and son.

The outstanding feature of Spence's career is his winning record: he has never lost a criminal trial and has not lost a civil trial in more than 30 years. Spence, the author of nine books, has also made frequent

appearances on television, both as a show host and a trial commentator.

Johnnie Cochran Jr.

The O. J. Simpson criminal trial brought several nationally known defense lawyers back into the spotlight. It also made household names of lawyers who until then had been prominent only in California, including prosecutors Marcia Clark and Christopher Darden. If any one legal professional came to be remembered as *the* lawyer associated with the "trial of the century," however, it was undoubtedly Johnnie Cochran Jr., who served as Simpson's lead defense counsel. Observers of the trial will long recall the alleged discrepancies in the prosecution's evidence,

Gerry Spence escorts his client Imelda Marcos, the former first lady of the Philippines, into the U.S. District Courthouse in Manhattan during her trial for racketeering. Marcos's acquittal was almost a sure thing: Spence has never lost a criminal trial.

"If it doesn't fit, you must acquit":
Johnnie Cochran during closing
arguments in the criminal trial
of O. J. Simpson.

which Cochran hammered home: "If it doesn't fit, you must acquit."

Longtime observers of Los Angeles judicial proceedings had known and respected Cochran as a savvy, formidable attorney for many years. A Louisiana native, he moved to Los Angeles to begin practicing law in 1963. He gained vast experience by trying cases on both sides of the courtroom, beginning as a criminal lawyer for the city of Los Angeles. Soon he formed a private practice and handled both criminal and civil cases. In the late 1970s, he again entered public service as assistant district attorney for Los Angeles County. Three years later, he formed another private practice, focusing on criminal defense and entertainment, personal injury, and public finance cases.

Throughout his career, Cochran earned many awards, including Criminal Trial Lawyer of the Year in Los Angeles. In 1994 he was listed among "the Best Lawyers in America."

When Simpson added him to the famous murder defense team, Cochran had already been noted as a defender and advocate in several high-profile cases. He successfully defended actor Todd Bridges against attempted-murder and assault charges in 1989. In 1993 singer Michael Jackson engaged Cochran to help defend him against allegations of sexual abuse of a minor; that case was settled out of court. And surprisingly, although Cochran's reputation was forged as a civil rights advocate and representative of minority clients, he took on the case of Reginald Denny, a white truck driver brutally beaten during race riots in Los Angeles in 1992. Denny and other plaintiffs contended in a civil suit that the city of Los Angeles had failed to provide ample police protection in the riot zone.

Cochran has been a longtime challenger of what he deems police injustices against minorities. He renewed that crusade at the Simpson trial. In closing arguments, he charged that the prosecution had presented false police testimony, and he admonished the jury to "stop this cover-up." The jury complied, finding Simpson not guilty in a surprisingly quick deliberation.

A popular author and speaker, Cochran today continues to campaign against police prejudice.

Alan M. Dershowitz

Famous defense lawyers have risen to prominence through very different paths. There is no formula for becoming one of the profession's foremost defense attorneys. Abe Lincoln split rails by day and "learned law" simply by poring over a law book by candlelight. F. Lee Bailey got the rudiments of a legal education in the U.S. Marines and learned to perform investigative work before he ever received a civilian law degree.

William Kunstler unraveled cipher messages for the army during World War II and planned to eventually become a writer; he was almost 30 by the time he obtained a law degree.

Alan M. Dershowitz, on the other hand, earned a reputation as one of the country's noted legal academicians early in his career. The Brooklyn, New York, native joined the Harvard Law School faculty when he was only 25; three years later he became the youngest full professor in the history of the prestigious law school.

Over the years, he has been called on to assist and advise defense counsel in various noteworthy cases. He was one of F. Lee Bailey's strategic advisers in the 1976 trial of Patty Hearst. Other celebrity clients have included boxer Mike Tyson and televangelist Jim Bakker, as well as entertainers and U.S. senators.

Dershowitz has insisted on upholding the constitutional rights of all citizens—even those whose aims and principles clash with his own. For example, he argued that members of the American Nazi Party were entitled to conduct a march in Illinois in 1977, although he is a longtime worker for Jewish causes. Dershowitz considers himself first and foremost a civil libertarian, and civil liberties such as the right of free speech, he argues, must be guaranteed to all.

In perhaps his best-known defense work, Dershowitz was asked to join the appeal process after the 1982 conviction of wealthy Rhode Islander Claus von Bulow for the attempted murder of the defendant's wife. Von Bulow was accused of injecting his wife, Sunny, with potentially lethal doses of insulin; she remained in a coma. Dershowitz's meticulous investigation raised suspicions that Sunny von Bulow's condition may have been her own doing. The state supreme court ordered a new trial, at which von Bulow was acquitted.

Leona Helmsley, a wealthy New York business tycoon, turned to Dershowitz in 1989 to help appeal

her conviction on multiple charges of tax evasion, mail fraud, conspiracy, and extortion. Five years later, Dershowitz became part of the so-called dream team of defense lawyers hired to represent O. J. Simpson.

Besides teaching law courses, Dershowitz has written books and articles and has lectured worldwide. His courses have covered a broad range of subjects, including criminal law, tactics and ethics in criminal litigation, human rights, civil liberties and violence, constitutional litigation, and psychiatry and law.

Dershowitz has been asked to appear before congressional committees studying legal issues and has won numerous awards. *Time* magazine probably best summarized Dershowitz's reputation when it described him as "the top lawyer of last resort in the country."

Harvard law professor Alan Dershowitz, one of the nation's top appellate attorneys, has been retained by a host of prominent clients.

DEFENSE
LAWYERS
AT WORK

Defense of a criminal client is not a haphazard process, even in small matters. In order to ensure a just outcome for a client, the lawyer must fully understand the case and spend time preparing the most effective defense possible.

Obviously, interviewing the client is essential. The lawyer must obtain every relevant detail about the client's involvement (if any) in the matter. In addition, the lawyer must determine if the client's statements are consistent with statements made to police or witnesses. Records must also be checked. If a criminal defendant or corporate client has a prior record of charges or complaints, the lawyer needs to know this.

Probation records can provide much of the basic information in criminal cases. But the lawyer may also need to know about the client's health, employment, and educational backgrounds. Does the client have a record of mental evaluation or treatment? The lawyer must know where these and other kinds of data can be found,

An effective defense begins with a careful, thorough interview of the client. The last thing a defense lawyer wants is a courtroom surprise.

49

and how to obtain the information as quickly as possible.

Meanwhile, the lawyer and staff gather all the information they can about the charge against their client. Even seemingly cut-and-dried cases may be open to challenge. To develop possible arguments in defense of the accused, the lawyer must learn as much as possible about what happened. Thorough trial teams often come to know more about the case than the client knows.

In certain kinds of cases, expert witnesses may be able to support the defendant's position. The lawyer must have a grasp of what kinds of expert resources are available and where to locate them. Typical expert witnesses are doctors who can testify about the nature of specific injuries, engineers or inspectors who can discuss automobile or structural design factors, and technology specialists knowledgeable in computer crimes and questions about electronic data. The prosecution is likely to call its own experts. The defense lawyer must also be alert to the kinds of testimony these witnesses may offer.

Lawyers and their staff may take depositions from both primary and secondary witnesses. Depositions are question-and-answer sessions held during the preparation for a trial. Although depositions are not part of trial proceedings in court (they usually take place in a lawyer's office), the witnesses are questioned under oath, and their statements are recorded by a court reporter or stenographer. What they say ("depose") during these sessions may be introduced in court—especially if a witness changes his or her story when questioned later at the trial. For both sides the great advantage of depositions is that they reveal in advance what various witnesses will likely disclose under oath in court. A popular saying among trial lawyers is "Never ask a witness a question before a jury unless you already know what the answer is going to be."

During case preparation, lawyers on both sides file motions for discovery. Through discovery a lawyer is entitled to copies of documents and other evidence possessed by the opposing side. In the past, no authorized

discovery process existed in the United States. Surprise evidence and surprise witnesses made many courtroom scenes quite dramatic. Thanks to the discovery system, which became common in the late 20th century, surprise elements in litigation are rare today. Theoretically, a lawyer can learn before trial what evidence the opposing side possesses, what witnesses it will call, and what statements the main witnesses have placed on record in depositions. Thus the trial process is not a contest marked by surprises, but one in which each lawyer relies on professional skills, knowledge, and diligence in presenting and refuting evidence and witnesses.

Before the case comes into the courtroom for trial, different pleadings and motions may be in order. Pleadings are formal papers filed with the court. A complaint is a pleading; the defendant's reply is a pleading. In submitting pleadings, each side states its case and describes the legal issues, as it sees them, for the benefit of the judge.

Motions are formal requests made by a lawyer to the

A defense lawyer reads from a document while the prosecutor listens from the witness stand during a pretrial evidentiary hearing. A good defense lawyer can win many cases before the trial even begins by getting the judge to exclude evidence damaging to his or her client.

judge. They're intended to improve the client's position—possibly even to win the case—before or during trial. In pretrial motions, for example, the defense lawyer may argue, "The prosecution has failed to offer sufficient evidence against my client. I move for dismissal of the case," or, "I respectfully ask the court to strike from evidence my client's previous record of alcohol-related arrests. They are irrelevant to the legal issues involved in the case at hand." Later, if the challenged evidence is permitted during the trial, the defense lawyer may interrupt the proceedings with a motion for a directed verdict of dismissal or acquittal, claiming the evidence is clearly insufficient to establish guilt.

It is the defense lawyer's job to ensure that the accused receives a fair trial. This part of the legal battle is waged primarily before the trial occurs.

The lawyer may sense that the case is so emotionally charged in the city or county where the charges have been filed that few jurors there would be likely not to have heard about it and formed suspicions and opinions. In this situation, the lawyer may file a motion requesting a change of venue for the upcoming trial. If the motion is granted, the trial is held in a distant locale where, it is hoped, prospective jurors will know little of the case and therefore can hear and evaluate the evidence objectively.

Sensational, inaccurate, and biased news and editorial coverage have marred criminal investigations and trials throughout America's history. In the national outrage following the 1932 kidnapping of aviator Charles Lindbergh's 19-month-old son, any adult accompanying a blond-haired toddler in the general vicinity of the crime was eyed suspiciously. When authorities arrested a suspect in the crime, Bruno Richard Hauptmann, more than two years later, his German nationality and previous criminal record inspired a general consensus that he was a "Nazi child killer" (the Lindbergh baby's body had since been found). Shouting spectators at Hauptmann's trial

The 1935 trial of Bruno Richard Hauptmann, accused of kidnapping and killing the son of aviator Charles Lindbergh, became a media circus. Here photographers use every available vantage point to snap a picture of Lindbergh (center, without hat) as he emerges from the courthouse in Flemington, New Jersey.

demanded that the jury burn the defendant, and reporters openly wagered on how long it would take jurors to reach a guilty verdict. It didn't take long to decide the question of guilt, and after deliberating only 11 hours, the jury recommended the death penalty. Hauptmann was executed on April 6, 1936.

Another famous instance of questionable media zeal was the trial and conviction of Dr. Sam Sheppard in Bay Village, Ohio, in 1954. Sheppard was accused of brutally murdering his wife, then injuring himself in order to deflect suspicion; he maintained that he had struggled with the real killer, a shaggy-haired intruder. Members of the media reported a possible love affair between the doctor and another woman, the inference being that this was the motive for the murder. They also suggested that Sheppard's well-to-do family had helped him destroy incriminating evidence. When Sheppard was convicted, one editor boasted that he was glad to have helped see justice done by demanding an aggressive investigation and prosecution.

New evidence presented 12 years later by trial lawyer F. Lee Bailey persuaded the U.S. Supreme Court to set aside Sheppard's conviction. "Massive, pervasive and prejudicial publicity," the Court ruled, had prevented the doctor from receiving a fair trial. The Court ordered a retrial, in which Sheppard was found innocent.

In addition to having an exhaustive knowledge of the law, the defense lawyer must be well acquainted with the court rules and procedures used in the jurisdiction where a case arises. At every turn, the lawyer must be alert in protecting the defendant's rights.

In a criminal matter, the burden of proof is on the state, or prosecution. Likewise, in a civil action, the burden of proof is on the plaintiff—the party who filed the complaint. Two things must be proved: 1) there was, in fact, a legal violation, and 2) the defendant was the violator. The defense lawyer's task is to expose weaknesses in the proof offered by prosecutors or attorneys for the plaintiff and to make sure that prosecutors and plaintiffs' attorneys operate within the rules of legal procedure in establishing their proof.

Establishing that a crime occurred is not commonly at issue once an arrest has been made—although this occasionally challenges law enforcement agencies. For example, the fact that a valuable object is reported missing from a home doesn't mean it was stolen, and the fact that a person disappears for months or years under suspicious circumstances doesn't mean a kidnapping or murder has been committed. An actual crime must be established before anyone can be charged.

Attorney F. Lee Bailey (right)
with his client Dr. Sam Sheppard.
Bailey succeeded in getting the
Supreme Court to overturn
Sheppard's murder conviction
because of "massive, pervasive
and prejudicial publicity."

Also difficult for the state to prosecute are *attempted* crimes that never come to pass. It is not against the law for someone to discuss a possible crime with friends, or even to plan it and make certain preparations for it. It is a crime, though, to attempt to carry it out, even if the attempted crime fails. Defense lawyers are diligent to distinguish between criminal *preparation* and criminal *attempt*. For example, if you publicly threaten to burn a building, buy a container of gasoline, and are seen with the container near the building but nothing more occurs, it may be difficult for a prosecutor to prove attempted arson. But if you proceed to pour gasoline around the premises and strike a match, and then someone intervenes before the gasoline ignites, your lawyer may have a much more difficult time defending you against a charge of attempted arson. Laws define criminal attempts as "overt acts"—not just preparations—toward committing crimes. Where is the line drawn? In some cases it may seem unclear.

The second requirement—proving that the defendant was the violator—is usually at the heart of criminal cases. If everyone agrees that a crime has occurred, the defense will usually be: "You've arrested the wrong suspect."

In certain situations even conclusive proof on both points may not result in conviction. The defense lawyer may be able to show that even though the defendant caused an injury to occur, certain circumstances—known as mitigating factors—made the occurrence unavoidable or at least partly justifiable. In those cases punishment may be reduced, if not eliminated.

More than a dozen varieties of mitigating factors are regularly argued in law courts. In criminal matters, these factors include:

- *Self-defense:* This argument is common in matters involving acts of violence. The killing or injuring of another person in order to preserve your own life has long been accepted as a defense by American courts.
- *Defending others:* Likewise, the killing or injuring of another person in order to preserve the life of a third party is defensible.
- *Consent:* This defense is sometimes offered in such criminal matters as rape (did intercourse take place with the woman's consent?) and kidnapping (did the alleged victim agree without force or threat to accompany the alleged kidnapper?).
- *Statute of limitations:* Laws provide that both criminal charges and civil grievances must be filed within a certain time after an alleged wrongdoing was committed. Different kinds of offenses carry statutes of limitations of varying durations. If the statute of limitations has passed when a charge or complaint is filed, the defense lawyer can argue that although his or her client may have perpetrated the wrongdoing, the client can no longer be prosecuted. Murder is a notable exception; it carries no statute of limitations. Long-unresolved murder cases have been brought to trial many years—in some cases, decades—after the crime occurred.

- *Double jeopardy:* A defendant cannot be tried twice for the same crime. This guarantee is stated in the Fifth Amendment to the U.S. Constitution.

As discussed earlier, professional football star O. J. Simpson was, in a sense, tried twice for the same crime. Was this double jeopardy? No. The first, and most sensational, trial—in 1995—was in criminal court, where he stood accused of the murders of his ex-wife, Nicole Brown Simpson, and her friend Ronald Goldman at Nicole's Los Angeles condominium. After Simpson's acquittal in the criminal trial, the families of the two victims filed civil complaints charging him with blame in their loved ones' "wrongful deaths." The families at that point could not seek to have Simpson convicted and imprisoned for murder, but they could win damage awards in civil court if they could prove he was responsible. They sued. In 1997, Simpson was found guilty after a five-month civil trial and was ordered to pay $33.5 million.

How could it be that the two different *Simpson* juries reached opposite verdicts? One major factor is that the stipulations for determining guilt are not the same in criminal and civil trials. In his book *Reasonable Doubts* (published after the criminal acquittal but before the civil verdict), Alan M. Dershowitz explained: "The burden of proof in a criminal case is 'beyond a reasonable doubt,' while the burden of proof in a civil case is 'by a mere preponderance of the evidence.' Simply put, this means that it takes more and better proof to convict a criminal defendant of a crime than to hold a civil defendant liable for monetary damages."

It is vital that a defense lawyer thoroughly understand the law as well as legal precedent—the way in which higher courts have ruled on identical or similar points of law in past cases. There are many pitfalls. Just as there are subtle, seemingly odd reasons why admitted wrongdoings may legally be excusable, there are other defense arguments that will not be accepted, even though on the surface they appear relevant and strong. To further complicate defense practice, since laws are different from state to state, certain defenses are valid in some jurisdictions but not others. The defense lawyer must know which arguments can be used and which can't—both universally and locally.

Not all evidence is admissible in court. Three types of evidence are frequently challenged by opposing lawyers at trial: 1) evidence that is hearsay, 2) evidence that is irrelevant to the charge at hand, and 3) evidence that is privileged. The defense lawyer must be careful to make sure a witness does not delve into any of the three forbidden areas.

Hearsay is evidence that is not based on a witness's direct knowledge but rather on another person's statement: "John told me Marianne told him she was making $200 a week dealing cocaine." Such information can't be presented to a jury. If John himself is questioned, *he* may testify: "Marianne told me she makes $200 a week dealing cocaine." But it is not permissible to offer as evidence a statement allegedly made to a third party. That's because in the process of human communication, statements are frequently rephrased and altogether misinterpreted.

Another reason hearsay testimony is disallowed is that the Sixth Amendment to the Constitution gives the accused the right to confront and question his or her accuser(s) in court. How can defendant Marianne (or her defense lawyer) confront accuser John if he's not in the courtroom—perhaps not even in the city, state, or country? If this damning statement is to be entered into evidence, it must be entered by John, not by a third party who didn't actually hear Marianne say it.

The second form of problematic evidence is the irrelevant statement or exhibit. A witness's revelation about the defendant may be absolutely true, it may be sensational, it may be unsavory, it may be extremely serious, and it may even implicate the defendant in another offense. But if it has nothing to do with proving a specific fact in the current matter, it's not relevant to the case at hand. Therefore, it is inadmissible.

The third category of inadmissible evidence is privileged information. The law recognizes that communication that occurs in the course of certain professional relationships—for example, the relationship between doctor and patient or lawyer and client—is not subject to disclosure in court. Thus, even if a client admitted to his lawyer that he committed a felony crime, the lawyer couldn't testify about that statement in court proceedings. Similarly, the courts have ruled that a Catholic priest to whom a murderer confessed can't be compelled to share that information with authorities because statements made in the confessional are considered privileged.

By knowing the intricacies of the law, legal precedent, and the rules of evidence—and by being able to accurately assess the strength of a prospective case—skillful defense attorneys frequently win acceptable resolutions for their clients without going before judges and juries. When a case does go to trial, however, the experience and skill of a defense attorney are put to the test in dramatic fashion.

A criminal court judge reviews documents during an evidentiary hearing. Certain types of evidence, such as hearsay, are inadmissible in court, and it's up to the defense lawyer to object to such evidence if the prosecution attempts to introduce it.

THE DEFENDANT'S DAY IN COURT

A defendant confers with his lawyer during the jury-selection phase of a trial. The ability to identify jurors who might be inclined to render a favorable verdict is a huge asset for a defense attorney.

After each side's legal counsel has assembled his or her evidence, and rulings have been handed down on pretrial motions, the lawyers present pretrial orders to the court. These documents list all the potential witnesses and itemize the exhibits the lawyers plan to offer into evidence.

The case is then ready for the trial process to begin. If the case will be decided by a judge or panel of judges with no jury, the plaintiff's attorney begins presenting his or her case. In jury trials the proceedings begin with the selection of a jury.

The defense lawyer must be especially diligent in questioning prospective jurors. Those who may harbor a bias, however small, against the defendant must be identified and excused from service. But beyond that, defense lawyers, like prosecutors, look for potential jurors who will be not simply impartial, but sympathetic to their side of the case. Veteran attorneys know that seating a favorable jury is both science and art.

Jury consultants, who are sometimes hired to advise lawyers during jury selection, can identify which groups of people will be more or less likely to respond sympathetically to a defendant accused of a particular crime. But good trial lawyers know that statistical probabilities aren't everything, and in questioning potential jurors they pay attention to subtle cues that may indicate whether or not the person would be inclined to render a favorable judgment in the case.

After the jurors have been selected and seated, the trial starts with the prosecutor (or plaintiff's lawyer) making an opening argument. Typically, this lawyer will summarize the allegations against the defendant and outline what proof of wrongdoing the prosecution intends to present in court. The defense lawyer then makes an opening argument, explaining how he or she intends to refute the charges. The defender may suggest alternate theories to explain what occurred or may point out that the evidence against the defendant is inconclusive.

The prosecutor then presents the case, introducing witnesses and entering documents and other exhibits for the court record. Placing a witness on the stand and interrogating him or her is called direct examination. After the prosecutor questions a witness, the defense lawyer has an opportunity to cross-examine that witness. When the cross-examination is done, the prosecutor has the chance to ask follow-up questions before the witness steps down. This stage of witness testimony is called redirect examination, and it becomes particularly important when the prosecutor believes that the defense lawyer has succeeded in damaging the witness's credibility or creating doubt or confusion about the witness's statements.

At the end of the prosecutor's presentation, the defense lawyer begins making the opposing case, calling witnesses and introducing evidence following the same process, with direct examination, cross-examination,

and redirect examination phases. If the defense counsel believes that the prosecution's case is weak and the issues are fairly simple for the jury to digest, the defender may make only a short presentation (hinting to the jury that he or she has little regard for the prosecution's case). If, on the other hand, the defender realizes that it will be hard to disprove vital parts of the charges, or if the issues are complex and the defender is concerned about the jury's understanding of the matter, the defense stage of the trial may take longer than the prosecution stage.

After all witnesses and exhibits have been presented, the opposing lawyers make their closing arguments, summarizing for the jury what they believe has been proved or disproved. The prosecution (or plaintiff) summarizes first, followed by the defense.

A defense attorney questions a witness at a murder trial in California. In the American courtroom, evidence is introduced through the direct examination, cross-examination, and redirect examination of witnesses.

In nonjury trials, the two sides present their cases in the same manner, seeking to persuade the judge or judges (the "court") directly. Depending on the nature of the crime, the complexity of surrounding issues, and the number of witnesses, presenting an entire case in this manner may take only a few minutes or it may take hours, days, even months.

In a jury trial, once the two sides have made their cases, the judge charges (instructs) the jury, clarifying the meaning and limitations of the law in question and the burden of proof. The jurors then go to the jury room to discuss and decide the case. Their deliberations may take minutes, hours, or days.

Arguing a case before a jury entails more than simply presenting facts. How the facts are presented—and how they are challenged—is often the deciding factor. Like it or not, lawyers are partly actors. They have to be. They know that jurors are observing their tone of voice, their gestures, their attitudes and emotions. Rightly or wrongly, a juror's impressions of a lawyer's courtroom personality, behavior, and comments can affect the verdict.

One of the most famous orators in American history, Daniel Webster, was a lawyer. He was credited with winning certain cases not through cleverness in examining witnesses or superior knowledge of the law (although he was a respected jurist), but largely on the strength of his courtroom speeches.

Lawyers have many ways of presenting and challenging evidence to cast it in a light more favorable to their side. Among their chief tactics is to "impeach" an opposing witness. In litigation terminology, to impeach is to discredit a witness in the minds of the jurors, thus weakening the potential damage of the person's testimony. This might be accomplished—perhaps subtly and sweetly, perhaps through a stern, rapid-fire line of questioning—by drawing from the witness a statement or suggestion

A witness breaks down on the stand. Such a display may have a powerful effect on jurors, but skillful defense lawyers can exploit more subtle witness reactions as well.

that contradicts a well-established fact or, better, something the witness has already said. It can also be effected by showing that a witness, although sincere and respectable, does not really know the facts.

There are other ways for a defense lawyer to use the witness's character or demeanor to advantage. For example, if a prosecution witness can be shown during questioning to be arrogant or aggressive, this may sway jurors' sympathies toward the defendant.

Another possible line of questioning might suggest that the witness is little more than a player in a game, a person who has been told exactly what to say by the opposing counsel and coached on how to say it, so that every statement seems almost robotic. Max Steuer, the defense lawyer in the Triangle Shirtwaist Company trial in December 1911, used this tactic to help win his case.

The Triangle Shirtwaist Company in New York City was one of the many sweatshops—factories where workers toiled long hours in dismal and often unsafe working conditions for meager wages—that existed in the United States a century ago. On March 25, 1911, a fire broke out in the eighth-floor workroom of the women's apparel manufacturer. The fire soon spread to Triangle's ninth-floor workroom. Workers there found their path to safety blocked by a door that had been locked from the outside to prevent employees from slipping away from their labors during work hours. Many faced a ghastly choice: plunge through the windows to the street far below, or stay inside and burn to death. Ultimately 146 Triangle employees perished; most were teenage girls hired to sew and cut cloth.

When the company's owners were charged with manslaughter and placed on trial later that year, the issue turned not on the question of whether the workroom door was locked (a fact no one disputed), but on whether the owners *knew* it was locked. Steuer raised doubt in the minds of jurors by getting a primary witness, one of the survivors, to state her testimony repeatedly; each time her words were practically verbatim. It was clear to the jury that the young woman had been drilled thoroughly by her lawyer. Ultimately Triangle's owners were acquitted.

Skillful litigators can put the steadiest of hostile witnesses off-balance. Even though this may not elicit an embarrassing statement, the resulting attitude of confusion or open resentment toward the questioner can lower a juror's opinion of the witness. Lawyers on the opposing side, however, may be able to restore the witness's credibility upon cross-examination or redirect examination by asking questions that put the witness at ease and clarify points of confusion in the testimony.

Criminal defense lawyers look for evidence that will demonstrate the human side of their client. Some of the most successful criminal defenders are those who can get the jury to look at the case through the defendant's eyes. They want the jury to be aware that the defendant—

whether innocent or guilty—is an individual just like everyone else, with thoughts and feelings, likes and dislikes, problems and interests.

In the infamous Lizzie Borden trial of 1893, defense lawyer George D. Robinson stressed in his closing argument the family "bond of union" between Lizzie Borden and her father, Andrew Borden, whom she was accused of murdering with an ax in order to secure a sizable inheritance. The father and daughter, Robinson argued, were far too close for Lizzie to be a serious suspect in the horrific murder. He pointed out that of all the items of jewelry the wealthy father could have worn from day to day, the lone item he chose to wear was a ring Lizzie had given him years before. Andrew Borden had literally gone to his grave wearing the ring. His daughter was acquitted.

Defending a client in court is, in a real sense, a matter of storytelling. That isn't to say it's something lawyers take lightly. Rather, in a case with complicated, interwoven legal issues, explaining those issues in "story form" is the only way lawyers can make sense of the information and the arguments for jurors with no legal education.

In their 1981 book, *Reconstructing Reality in the Courtroom*, W. Lance Bennett and Martha S. Feldman noted:

> Even lawyers and judges who receive formal legal training must rely on some commonsense means of presenting legal issues and cases in ways that make sense to jurors, witnesses, defendants, and spectators. . . . The story is an everyday form of communication that enables a diverse cast of courtroom characters to follow the development of a case and reason about the issues in it. Despite the maze of legal jargon, lawyers' mysterious tactics, and obscure court procedures, any criminal case can be reduced to the simple form of a story.

Witnesses as well as lawyers are storytellers in the courtroom. Not only does the storytelling technique

Defense attorney Leslie Abramson discusses a bloody shirt. Legal commentators have observed that arguing a case in court is about storytelling—constructing a plausible version of events that supports a particular point of view.

help jurors understand each piece of the trial puzzle, but it can also be vital in bringing all the pieces together.

Of course, lawyers and their witnesses hope to accomplish more than just simplifying the case for the jury and judge; they want to cast it in a light favorable to their side. Bennett and Feldman observed that the storyteller or "actor" in a trial "can re-present an episode in a version that conforms with his or her perspective both during and after the incident."

Does this mean that all storytellers are deceivers? Not necessarily. We all see everything in life through a personal lens. Our diverse experiences and understandings help shape what each new action means to us, how we will remember it, and how we will interpret it for others. The fact that two different commentators may retell the same story in very different ways—with both remaining sincere in their perspective—can be shown in ordinary sports coverage. One broadcast commentator may attribute a touchdown in football to fancy footwork by the ball carrier; another may cite a breakdown in the defense.

One consideration defense lawyers must bear in mind is that different people don't always hear and interpret the same story the same way. A sophisticated, upper-class juror, for example, may not fully appreciate the "street talk" of a particular witness. A working-class juror, on the other hand, may have trouble grasping the exact meaning or implications of testimony by a hospital administrator that explains the reasoning and regulations behind the facility's arrangements with insurance companies. A comment by a witness may elicit scowls from some jurors and chuckles or sympathy from others.

In the end, this can affect the jury verdict. As Bennett and Feldman wrote, "Jurors who come from different social worlds may disagree about the meaning and the plausibility of the same stories. . . . Stories that elicit different interpretations are among the most painful things to observe in the courtroom. When the defense manages to construct a plausible story only to discover that the jury lacks the experience necessary to understand it, the stark reality of injustice becomes clear."

Court challenges and the need for legal defenders are as old as America. Some of our earliest defense lawyers handled bizarre cases ranging from chicken theft to inappropriate tobacco spitting. They also handled serious cases—murder, embezzlement, armed robbery—that differ little from charges filed in the 21st century.

An early defense of national prominence was the trial of Aaron Burr. A controversial political figure, Burr distinguished himself in the patriot cause during the American Revolution, served in the U.S. Senate, was elected vice president under Thomas Jefferson, killed statesman and rival Alexander Hamilton in a duel, and in 1807 found himself on trial for treason. His accusers believed he was scheming either to invade Mexico and make it part of the fledgling United States—without authorization—or to organize and lead the southwestern territory (perhaps combined with Mexico) as a new, separate nation.

Burr chose as his defense lawyer Charles Lee, a former U.S. attorney general. In arguments before the Supreme Court, Lee won his client's acquittal. Burr lived the rest of his life in disgrace—but Lee earned a place in legal history as one of America's first high-profile defense lawyers.

Countless courtroom dramas from then till now have captured the public's interest and put defense counsel to the test. A classic example is the 1893 trial, mentioned above, of Lizzie Borden in Fall River, Massachusetts. She was a 32-year-old woman accused of murdering her aging father and stepmother, with whom she lived. Quite a bit of circumstantial evidence pointed to her guilt:

- She was known to dislike her stepmother and to fear that the stepmother—rather than Lizzie and her sister—would inherit most of the family property. (Lizzie and her sister afterward inherited a fortune.)
- She had tried to buy prussic acid, a highly toxic substance, the day before the crime (the druggist had refused to sell it to her).
- She was locked inside the house with the victims during the hour and a half in which the murders were committed—but claimed she heard nothing unusual.
- She burned the dress she'd been wearing on the morning of the murders, saying it had been stained with brown paint.
- She substantially changed her statements to the police during the investigation.

Accused murderer Lizzie Borden and her lawyer, George D. Robinson, in court, 1893. Borden's still-controversial acquittal probably resulted in part from good work by Robinson and in part from the unconcealed sympathy of a judge.

The fact that neither the police nor the defense could introduce any other serious suspects seemed to be another point against her. But at trial Lizzie's lawyers pointed out that it was not their obligation to find an alternative suspect. They also succeeded in having some of the evidence barred from the trial. Lizzie Borden was found innocent in a verdict that is still disputed by historians.

An interesting aspect of the *Borden* case was the

undisguised sympathy for the defendant that one of the judges displayed when he instructed the jury. Like many Borden sympathizers, he voiced doubt that such a crime could have been committed by a woman who was a regular churchgoer. Critics believed his statements might have prejudiced the jury.

Judges in generations past—and sometimes even today—are frequently accused by the losing side of influencing a verdict, either by favoring the opposition when ruling on motions or by making biased statements when instructing the jury. The Borden trial is an instance of a judge apparently favoring the defense. On the other side of the coin are cases such as the 1935 Lindbergh kidnapping trial. During jury instructions the judge reviewed some of defendant Bruno Hauptmann's claims and asked the jurors incredulously, "Do you believe *that?*" Even Charles Lindbergh, the slain child's father, reportedly told friends he thought the judge's comments were unfair.

The 1921 trial of Nicola Sacco and Bartolomeo Vanzetti is another illustration of a judge apparently favoring the prosecution. The defendants were immigrants from Italy who spoke only broken English. Their alleged crime: the April 1920 robbery of a shoe factory payroll in South Braintree, Massachusetts, and the murder of two company officials during the robbery.

Witnesses described the culprits as "foreign-looking." In America during those years—shortly after the Communist revolution in Russia—European immigrants were held in suspicion. Many Americans feared the rise of Communist organizations bent on revolution in this country. Several weeks after the crime, a policeman aboard a streetcar arrested Sacco, a shoe factory worker, and Vanzetti, a fish seller. The men were jailed without being told the charges against them. They were later indicted for the robbery and murder.

Their trial lasted six weeks. The defendants admitted they were radicals who opposed U.S. government

policies and labor practices. They had obviously lied to police when questioned about the pistols they carried (carrying side arms was not uncommon in those years) and about their association with political activists. But some of the prosecution's witnesses also changed their testimony. And the defense was able to undermine key physical evidence, including a ballistics expert's link between Sacco's gun and one of the fatal bullets, and a cap Sacco had supposedly left at the crime scene.

Guilty verdicts were reached quickly. But during the appeals process, which lasted six years, sympathizers of the defendants raised astonishing legal issues. For example:

Bartolomeo Vanzetti (center) and Nicola Sacco (right) with a guard. In 1921 the two admitted anarchists were convicted of robbery and murder—despite the fact that defense lawyers had discredited key physical evidence offered by the prosecution.

- The trial judge was quoted as boasting of the "anarchist" conviction. Just as alarmingly, in denying appeals for a retrial, he apparently helped justify his refusals by pointing to testimony that had never been introduced officially in the original trial.
- The jury foreman reportedly told a friend that the defendants should be punished regardless of their involvement in the robbery and shooting because they were "Reds," or radicals.
- A criminal later imprisoned for a different crime confessed to the robbery and shooting.
- An eyewitness who had identified the defendants in court subsequently withdrew her statement.
- The prosecution allegedly suppressed vital evidence that might have damaged the case against Sacco and Vanzetti.

The two men were sent to the electric chair in August 1927, still protesting their innocence. Half a century after their executions, a Massachusetts governor granted them a posthumous pardon in order to clear the record. Most legal historians agree that Sacco and Vanzetti should never have been convicted—at least not on the evidence produced at their trial.

Virtually any defense lawyer today would appeal such a case. And today the chances of winning a new trial—if not outright dismissal of the charges—would be much improved because of laws and court decisions strengthening defendants' rights.

Mistakes by the prosecution or the court may compel a losing defendant to appeal. In addition to new cases pending trial or negotiation, defense lawyers may have one or several cases in the appeals process. Those cases will be heard by an appellate court. If the appellate court upholds the negative decision of the lower court, the defendant may appeal to the state supreme court—but the supreme court is selective about the cases it will actually review.

Often a defendant may choose to engage a different

lawyer for the appeals process—or add to the defense team a lawyer who specializes in appeals work. The appeals procedure is quite different from the original court trial. An appeal before a higher court is not a retrial of the entire case; rather, it is a contesting of one or more specific aspects of the original trial that, in the view of the defense lawyer, were decided incorrectly in the lower court. A defense lawyer who performs brilliantly in the question-and-answer drama of a courtroom may not be especially knowledgeable in the more technical realm of appeals arguments before a panel of judges.

WHITE-COLLAR DEFENDERS

Michael Milken, a junk-bond financier accused of fraud and racketeering, leaves court with his legal team. The strategy for defending a white-collar criminal like Milken differs markedly from the strategy for defending a street criminal.

Violent crimes often result in spectacular and highly publicized court cases. Another type of crime that is much less visible to the public, though enormously damaging to society, became rampant during the last half of the 20th century. Representing its defendants are lawyers with special knowledge and skills. These are the white-collar defenders.

White-collar crimes—such as tax evasion, bribery, embezzlement, corporate price-fixing, stock market fraud, the misuse of public funds, and mail-order con schemes—don't use force or the threat of force and are typically committed by middle- and upper-class professionals (people whose work attire would traditionally include a white shirt with button-down collar). This area of lawbreaking was studied by sociologist Edwin H. Sutherland during the 1930s and 1940s. Sutherland was reportedly inspired to campaign against such violations after a Chicago utility tycoon was acquitted in a mail fraud and embezzlement case in 1934.

White-collar crimes have occurred since the nation's early history. Among many examples, the presidential administration of Warren G. Harding in the 1920s is remembered, sadly, more for its corruption than for anything it accomplished. Albert Fall, President Harding's secretary of the interior, was convicted of bribery in a scheme to lease government lands to oil companies without competitive bidding. The U.S. attorney general and the head of the Veterans' Bureau were disgraced for illegal profiteering and stealing from the government, respectively. Stress from the scandals is suspected of contributing to Harding's failing health and death in office.

Such crimes are not the exclusive domain of government officials, of course. They occur on a personal level and at every level of business. It was during the 1960s and 1970s, author Kenneth Mann points out, that "these crimes came to be identified as a major social problem. It is now conventional wisdom that they cause the loss of billions of dollars a year to the public, which is victimized by individual swindlers and by corporations and corporate officers carrying out complex schemes of deception."

A used-car salesman who resets odometers to deceive buyers about a vehicle's history is a white-collar criminal. So is the individual who exaggerates business losses in Internal Revenue Service filings in order to reduce tax liability. So is the corporation president who hides company profits in foreign bank accounts for the same purpose. Occasionally a person convicted of such a violation is sentenced to prison time. Usually, though, the sentence is a fine, often with restitution—the requirement to reimburse government, businesses, or private victims for any losses they incurred. The most damaging punishment may be the ruining of the criminal's image and career.

Although some lawyers competently defend both white-collar and non-white-collar cases, those who are

Albert Fall, former secretary of the interior during the Harding administration, leaves court after being sentenced to one year in jail and being ordered to pay a $100,000 fine for bribery.

interested in white-collar laws and violations typically focus on that realm. There is much to understand about the complexities of business operations and business law. Detailed knowledge of finance and accounting practices is essential. Rather than confronting and negotiating with criminal prosecutors, the defenders must often deal with investigators from different branches of government: the U.S. Treasury and state tax agencies, the Securities and Exchange Commission, the Federal Trade Commission, the Social Security Administration, and so on.

The fundamental defense strategy in a white-collar case often differs from that in other areas of law. The objective in "street crime" defense is usually to plea-bargain for the least severe sentence possible. The objective of the white-collar defender, on the other hand, is to clear the client or arrange a settlement before charges are ever filed. Much of the white-collar defender's work is done not after a client has been arrested, but during the government investigation. If possible, the lawyer will prevent the public embarrassment and possible loss of position that a formal charge would bring to the client.

Interestingly, the white-collar criminal defense lawyer engages not so much in protecting innocent clients as in helping guilty ones. Kenneth Mann observes, "The white-collar crime defense attorney, like his counterpart handling street crime, typically assumes that his client is guilty." Defenders of white-collar offenders may be able to coach their clients effectively in dealing with government investigators. They may be able to convince investigators that prosecution will be futile for lack of evidence.

First and foremost, they try to establish what Mann calls "information control." Successful information control, he explains, "keeps the government ignorant of evidence it needs in deciding whether to make a formal charge." Information control, considered neither illegal nor unethical, is simply part of the defense lawyer's stock-in-trade. The lawyer might argue that certain evidence is inadmissible because investigators did not follow the letter of the law in obtaining it. He or she might contend that a request for certain additional information would create an undue burden on the client.

Care must be taken to conduct this defense within legal bounds, obviously. Lawyers are forbidden by ethics rules to conceal certain kinds of information that the law requires or to advise clients to act illegally. They are also forbidden to lie to investigators. But they can and must, in their clients' interests, make sure investigators follow the rules and obtain only information to which they are entitled.

One unnerving pitfall in legal defense, especially common in white-collar cases, is possible secret nondisclosure by the client. A client might hide important information from his or her defense lawyer—information that investigators might ultimately obtain. This can undermine the lawyer's work and, in the end, destroy the case.

At the same time, defense lawyers don't always *want* to know certain things about the client or the case. "If an attorney believes that it will be useful to a possible defense strategy not to be informed by the client of everything the client knows," Mann writes, "he can simply not inquire. . . . [A]ttorneys are aware that they may get more information than is good for the defense position."

This complicated relationship among white-collar violators, their lawyers, and investigators does nothing to improve the overall reputation of defense counsel among critics. Indeed, high-level white-collar crimes— crimes of the rich and famous—draw special disdain from critics of the criminal justice system. In his book *Crime and Punishment in American History*, law professor Lawrence M. Friedman writes: "White-collar criminals, after all, are typically richer than the average street criminal. They can hire better lawyers; they are more sophisticated and articulate. . . . What may help [their activities] even more is the general perception that they are 'not really criminals,' that their acts are 'not really crimes.'"

PUBLIC DEFENDERS

Notorious serial killer Ted Bundy (center) with Ed Harvey, the public defender assigned to help represent him. Unlike defense lawyers in private practice, public defenders can't choose their clients.

Working at the other end of the social spectrum is a breed of comparatively low-paid, unheralded defenders who advocate for a very different kind of client. Public defenders are lawyers who devote their efforts to representing clients who cannot afford private counsel.

The right of an accused person to "the Assistance of Counsel" is guaranteed by the Sixth Amendment to the U.S. Constitution. But what if a defendant cannot *afford* a lawyer?

Only in the latter part of the 20th century did the U.S. judicial system deal with that question fully. For almost two centuries it was left to individual judges to decide whether an indigent, or poor, defendant required a lawyer in order to ensure a fair trial or plea agreement. Typically, free lawyer services were provided only in cases involving the most serious felonies or federal offenses.

In 1932, the U.S. Supreme Court began reversing

certain convictions in which defendants were believed to have had little or no legal counsel. In 1963 the high court ruled that a defense lawyer was necessary in order for a defendant to "be assured of a fair trial." Nine years later the Supreme Court reinforced the directive: all defendants in any type of case have a right to legal representation.

The 1963 case *Gideon v. Wainwright* is one of the most important in the movement to ensure defendants' rights. Clarence Earl Gideon was a Florida man arrested, tried, convicted, and sentenced to five years for breaking into a pool hall. Gideon had a long burglary record and had spent much of his life in prison. In this instance, though, he vehemently insisted that he was innocent. (Interestingly, he was an employee at the pool hall.) Lacking money to hire a lawyer, he demanded that the court get one for him. The local judge denied the demand, stating that counsel for indigents could be assigned only in capital offenses. Gideon, thus forced to defend himself, lost the jury verdict.

At that point in history, the trial judge was not without justification in denying Gideon a lawyer. Gideon based his argument on the Sixth Amendment, which guarantees a person's right to legal counsel—but in federal court, not necessarily in state jurisdictions.

What struck a chord of sympathy with the public and with judicial observers in Gideon's case was his crude and pitiable, but determined, effort to obtain justice for himself. Perhaps more fervent than his innocent plea was his anger at being denied legal counsel. From prison he wrote letters to courts in pencil on notebook paper. When his appeals reached Washington, the United States Supreme Court agreed to review his case and appoint a lawyer to represent him. The lawyer was Abe Fortas—who would himself later become a Supreme Court justice.

The *Gideon* case was clearly breaking new ground. In order to rule in Gideon's favor, the Supreme Court would have to expand markedly the concept of every defendant's right to counsel. To Fortas, the right to counsel was at issue not only in the Sixth Amendment, but also in the Fourteenth. In part, that amendment guarantees "due process of law" for everyone in every state of the Union. Further, it commands that each state provide "within its jurisdiction the equal protection of the laws." Due process of law, Fortas stressed, could not result without a fair trial; a fair trial could not be assured without competent legal representation. And equal protection of the laws meant that competent legal representation must be provided to every defendant, including those who cannot afford to hire a lawyer.

The high court agreed, rejecting the state of Florida's argument that each state has the authority to decide in which criminal cases lawyers should be appointed for poor defendants. Gideon was granted a new trial with a capable lawyer and was acquitted. More important, the Supreme Court ruling would affect millions of cases across the land in the coming years. Right away the cases of more than 4,000 other Florida prison inmates had to be retried; about half of the defendants went free.

Gideon v. Wainwright bore out the long-stated contention of Justice Hugo Black: "There can be no equal justice where the kind of trial a man gets depends on the amount of money he has." Court critics maintain that rich defendants with high-priced lawyers still have a better chance of winning acquittal or light sentencing than poor clients or defendants of average financial means. Even some observers who agreed with O. J. Simpson's acquittal in his 1995 criminal trial raised questions about how the victory was obtained. Simpson hired not one high-profile, high-priced defense lawyer, but a whole team of them, as well as forensic experts. If he had been less potently represented, might he have lost the case? What of the countless defendants who cannot afford to hire a private lawyer at all, much less the "best" lawyer? Despite the criticism, few would deny that thanks to Clarence Earl Gideon's persistence, the lot of

This page: Clarence Gideon, whose appeal of his conviction for breaking into a pool hall with the intent to commit burglary changed the American justice system. Opposite page: Abe Fortas, chosen by the U.S. Supreme Court to represent Gideon, successfully argued that the Constitution guarantees all indigent defendants the right to a court-appointed lawyer.

underprivileged defendants has improved dramatically.

As a result of such landmark decisions, a special kind of defense lawyer has come to greater prominence in America's judicial system: the public defender. Public defenders were not "invented" as a result of *Gideon*; they had already been at work for generations in America's courts. Salaried by local governments, public defenders do not work for standard legal fees, nor do they select their clients, as private lawyers do. They are appointed by the courts.

Some counties in America have only one public defender, perhaps with one or two assistants. The

nation's largest counties, on the other hand, have hundreds of public defenders. Each lawyer is likely to be assigned dozens of cases a year.

In many counties public defenders are bright, young lawyers eager to obtain criminal law experience and fight for social justice. Other public defenders are veterans with many years at the bar. Although many indigent defendants are skeptical of the quality of their lawyers' skills ("I didn't have a lawyer; I had a public defender" is a modern adage among prison inmates), statistics indicate that some public defenders are among the best defense lawyers in America.

Public defenders are expected to work just as hard for their clients as private lawyers do for paying clients. Even if an indigent client pleads or is proved guilty, he or she has a right to expect proper treatment and fair sentencing. The public defender must ensure that this is provided. In the case of a first-time offender who pleads guilty to a nonviolent crime, the lawyer will usually seek a nonprison sentence and rehabilitation to help the defendant avoid future trouble.

Public defender offices are also staffed with investigators who can search for evidence with the defendant's interests in mind. Often the investigator will personally visit the scene of a crime or incident to get a full understanding of what happened.

Although lawyers working as public defenders could earn much higher incomes representing paying clients, many find their work rewarding in other ways. They know they are performing a service that is vital in a democracy.

Janice Fukai, a public defender in Los Angeles County, California, explained: "[W]hat would it be like if only some people charged with crimes were entitled to free counsel? Who would have the godlike power to decide who is worth defending and who is not? Public defenders are committed to justice for all." Incidentally, in 1914 Los Angeles County became the first county in the nation to create a public defender system. It is considered one of the most effective in the country.

Many public defenders work long hours not only to shepherd their clients through the legal system, but to help them become productive members of society afterward. Gary Horton, a public defender in Genesee County, New York, is part of an innovative team approach to criminal justice in his jurisdiction. The Genesee Justice Program strives to identify offenders who are genuinely sorry for their crimes and to help them "earn back their place in the community." Rather than imprison certain offenders for long periods, the program sentences them to public service tasks, imposes restrictions and special assignments on juveniles, and provides other means of diverting offenders from a life of crime. Sometimes the offenders sit down and discuss their actions with their victims.

"Because we're public defenders doesn't mean we don't want to see a safe community or that we don't want to see victims protected or a jail not overcrowded," Horton told a magazine interviewer. "But we also want to see programs that give our clients an opportunity, presuming they have offended, to break the cycle they're in and avoid re-offending in the future."

A Board
Game for
Bureaucrats?

T he public defender is clearly a vital figure in the modern American criminal justice system. At the same time, in the minds of some observers this type of lawyer is but one more player in a system that has strayed from its noble mission.

Some critics view court proceedings as mere contests. Lawyers are the players; judges are the referees; the law is the set of rules by which the "game" is played. The defendant might be likened to a token in a board game, or perhaps to the pigskin in football. Monopoly players are never trying to win the game on behalf of their token—the iron or the steamboat or the car—they are in it for themselves. They don't represent their token; their token represents them. Meanwhile, football and basketball players care nothing about "punishing" or "acquitting" the ball; their objective is to win the game that is being played *around* the ball.

In this sense, a defendant in a criminal trial might be viewed as a token in the board game called Court

Courtroom drama: Cynics have argued that all the major players in a trial know they are performing for the benefit of the jury.

Procedures. While the defense lawyer in theory represents the defendant, it's also the other way around—the defendant represents the lawyer's track record in this game of legal intelligence and skill.

At the same time, another game seems to be going on: a game of charades, in which everyone participates. In a typical courtroom scene, prosecutor and defense lawyer spar with visible hostility. The prosecutor exhibits no doubt that the accused is truly guilty; the defense lawyer seems equally convinced of the person's innocence. The professional combatants shout and sneer at each other and at opposing witnesses. They glare, roll their eyes in mock disgust, and disparage the opponent's case.

Interestingly, these opposing lawyers may be old friends—whose friendship will in no way be diminished by the trial at hand. Many defense lawyers begin their careers as prosecutors, and vice-versa. "Close and continuing relations between the [defense lawyer] and his former colleagues in the prosecutor's office," writes law and sociology professor Abraham S. Blumberg, "generally overshadow the relationship between the [lawyer] and his client. . . . Indeed, the adversary features which are manifest are for the most part muted and exist . . . largely for external consumption."

The lawyers are basically actors—and so is the defendant. In his book *Criminal Justice,* Blumberg writes that in plea bargaining "the organizational structure of the criminal court . . . gives [the accused] the stage directions of his role performance." In this "charade," he says, "an accused must project an appropriate and acceptable degree of guilt, penitence, and remorse. If he adequately feigns the role of the 'guilty person,' his hearers will engage in the fantasy that he is contrite and thereby merits a lesser plea. One of the essential functions of the criminal lawyer is that he coach his accused-client in this performance. . . . Everyone present is aware of the staging, including the defendant."

Defense lawyers point out that they are *required* to be vigorous advocates for the accused. In his book *The Trial Lawyer's Art*, author Sam Schrager observes that America's adversarial justice system "requires lawyers to show zealous allegiance to their side's version of truth. The need to be believable to jurors pushes lawyers well beyond giving a straightforward presentation of evidence. It forces them to try to create the *appearance* of truth."

Schrager is a professor who, in conjunction with the Smithsonian Institution, has studied trials as "folkloric" performances. He spent day after day observing court proceedings, concluding that a jury trial, "from beginning to end, is an artfully performed event. From the moment opposing counsels first appear before prospective jurors until the moment the verdict is in, they are performing. They must."

Schrager did not condemn this process. He explained that a courtroom performance is not a show of "trickery, with the lawyer mounting a show he or she knows to be

A prosecutor and a defense attorney chat during a recess in a murder trial. Despite the adversarial demeanor they display for jurors inside the courtroom, opposing attorneys are often friends.

false," but instead is "a skilled display of communication that holds an audience, stimulates their senses, provokes their emotions."

Naturally, some lawyers are better "actors" than others. If the adage "You get what you pay for" applies here, does it suggest that a defendant's guilt or innocence, in the eyes of the law, depends on his or her ability to hire the best "actor"? It's one of many questions skeptics raise about the game of criminal law.

The best answer to that question may be neither "yes" nor "no," but "in part." Certainly some defense lawyers have better win-loss trial records than others, and presumably their abilities and knowledge have something to do with that. But in their book *Reconstructing Reality in the Courtroom*, authors W. Lance Bennett and Martha S. Feldman point out that "it is a mistake to carve out the lawyer as a unit of analysis" among all the players in criminal court trials. Furthermore, "it is simplistic to explain the effectiveness of lawyers in narrow terms of oratory, charismatic presence, or legal knowledge. Effectiveness is more a function of whether these and other resources can be employed selectively at critical junctures in the development of the overall story about a crime."

Abraham Blumberg, in a law journal article titled "The Practice of Law as Confidence Game," observed that although lawyers have a duty to their clients, they also have a duty to the court. The court is a form of bureaucracy. Defense lawyers, Blumberg wrote, sometimes find themselves "abandoning their ideological and professional commitments to the accused client" and serving, first and foremost, the "court organization." He noted, "Accused persons come and go in the court system schema, but the structure and its occupational incumbents remain to carry on their respective career, occupational and organizational enterprises." "Occupational incumbents" include lawyers, judges, and other court officials.

"Lawyer regulars"—defense lawyers who represent

Symbols of justice adorn the courtroom, but some critics charge that the legal system primarily serves lawyers, judges, and other legal professionals.

most criminal cases—are virtual fixtures of criminal court, Blumberg suggested. "[T]heir offices line the back streets of the courthouses, at times sharing space with bondsmen. Their political 'visibility' in terms of local club house ties, reaching into the judge's chambers and prosecutor's office, are also deemed essential to successful practitioners." He described the court as "a closed community" and decried the "inherent deficiencies of assembly line justice, so characteristic of our major criminal courts."

In short, according to Blumberg, "regular" defense lawyers mainly operate not as independent agents interested only in their clients' rights and protections, but as members of the court bureaucracy. What happens if the two roles clash? "The client, then," Blumberg wrote, "is a secondary figure in the court system as in certain other bureaucratic settings. He becomes a means to other ends of the organization's incumbents."

As in most bureaucracies, inadequate funding, resources, and time pose serious problems for criminal courts. Courts are under tremendous pressure to process a high volume of cases. But genuine "due process" of every case would take more time than a court can give. Result: defendants are strongly encouraged to plea-bargain rather than go to trial. Lawrence M. Friedman has labeled this "bargained justice."

Friedman observed that the concept of plea bargaining came under attack from opposite directions in the 1970s. Liberals howled that plea bargaining had become "barbaric: a defendant's fate was decided by haggling, not by an honest trial." Conservatives took the opposite view: "Hardened criminals, adept at playing the game, bargained for a 'slap on the wrist.'"

Another factor in the so-called game of criminal justice is payment. Lawyers perform a vital role in the American judicial system and serve a dignified purpose, but in the process they have to make a living. Cynics often point out that many a lawyer makes an extremely good living.

Public defenders are paid by the government to represent indigent clients. "Regular" defense lawyers, on the other hand, are paid by their clients, or their clients' families and friends. Blumberg wrote that lawyers who defend robbers are sometimes paid their fee from the spoils of the crime—and are undoubtedly aware of it. In fact, he observed, "the amount of the [lawyer's] fee is a function of the dollar value of the crime committed, and is frequently set with meticulous precision at a sum which bears an uncanny relationship to that of the net proceeds of the particular offense involved." He added that criminals released on bail have been known to commit thefts in order to pay their lawyers.

No lawyer would openly acknowledge accepting contraband as payment, of course. As for demanding handsome fees from criminal defendants, most defenders can make a strong argument that they deserve substantial fees for their substantial legal services.

But what has clearly happened, according to Blumberg, is that criminal law practice has evolved into a callous bureaucracy. What has become most important is not that every defendant receives real justice, but that the system works as smoothly as possible and compensates all the legal professionals involved for their work. The defendant is almost relegated to the role of bystander while being "processed" through plea bargaining.

Blumberg noted that criminal defenders have three main tasks: 1) to make sure they will be paid, 2) to prepare their defendants emotionally for the possibility of defeat, and 3) to perform "adequately" in negotiating the case through the court process. In such a scenario the relationship between defendant and defense lawyer is rarely a friendly one. Simple statistics appear to bear that out: criminal cases are usually plea-bargained without going to trial, and prison inmates usually insist either that they are innocent or that they should have gotten a better deal in plea bargaining. Many convicted criminals, Blumberg said, view the court system as a "monstrous organizational apparatus" and tend to plead to lesser crimes simply to end their legal ordeals.

On the other hand, judicial experts generally recognize that most criminal defendants are guilty, despite their denials. Rather than go to prison for crimes they didn't commit, they're more likely to "get off light," serving relatively short sentences after plea bargaining.

Still, even if only a handful of convicted defendants really are innocent or are less guilty than their sentences call for, critics of the bureaucracy contend that something is wrong with the U.S. criminal court system. The court bureaucracy, they suggest, may be more important than justice itself.

"The adversary system," Blumberg lamented, "has always been an ideal goal at best."

CHANGES AND CHALLENGES

T he early American court system little resembled the vast, diverse judicial network we have today. When the colonies were under British dominion, ordinary cases were heard in local courts—which were also responsible for collecting taxes and managing other governmental affairs. The courthouse (in cities that had such a building dedicated to judicial and government business) naturally became a public gathering place. Besides observing courtroom proceedings, citizens came from all around to talk politics, discuss current events, and share news and rumors.

Cases that were not resolved in local courts went to superior courts. Superior court justices often included government officials, sometimes governors. Colonial legislatures functioned as the highest courts of appeal.

Many of our early lawyers were not well trained. Abraham Lincoln, as we've seen, never had a formal education beyond a few months of reading, writing, and

Technology is changing the face of American courtrooms, not only by facilitating record keeping but also by allowing lawyers to present sophisticated graphics to help jurors understand the evidence.

arithmetic at log cabin schools. But he educated himself by reading at home, usually by dim candlelight in the evenings. He became a crafty "country lawyer" and eventually one of the world's greatest leaders.

In the 20th century, many American lawyers still were not noted for their law school credentials. Clarence Darrow, one of the most famous lawyers in the nation's history, studied law for only one year before entering practice. Some of our early judges lacked legal training and were sometimes appointed out of popularity or political favoritism.

Today lawyers are highly trained in (typically) three-year law school programs. Judges possess the same training plus exceptional evaluative and leadership skills and, in most instances, years of experience. Continuing education is encouraged and often required among legal professionals.

And just as the space-age, digital world of today little resembles the world of our founders, the lawyer's office and courtroom today little resemble those of our ancestors. By using technology to full advantage, lawyers are steadily improving the overall quality of the nation's justice system.

Jurors of yesteryear often had to battle to keep their eyes open during long, roundabout testimony by expert witnesses who spoke in strange terminology. Today jurors get full-color, three-dimensional animations that illustrate exactly what the expert is talking about. Nowadays trials are visual affairs—and computer graphics are an essential item in the defense lawyer's toolbox. Dr. Jo-Ellan Dimitrius, a trial consultant and author, likens today's visual courtroom to the age-old game of show-and-tell. In generations past, litigators like Darrow relied on their verbal skills to win cases. That alone won't suffice today against a powerful visual presentation by opposing counsel. "The visual stimulation for jurors is so very important," Dimitrius has observed. "What we've learned is that we can't just rely upon the oratory."

Legal teams don't prepare pictures alone. Computer programs can generate sound and video, and combine them with other elements. Michael R. Arkfeld, a nationally known lawyer in Phoenix, Arizona, observed, "Once you digitize it, you control the information." He added that in modern trials, jurors have come to *expect* lawyers to use helpful visual and audio aids.

Defense lawyers use computers not just to "wow" a jury with impressive, convincing graphics, but to provide quick, thorough searches for needed information and to manage the case. They also use them for legal research.

Legal research involves two things: 1) a thorough scrutiny of the law, coupled with a search for similar cases that have already been decided and entered into various court records, and 2) a search for any kind of information that might shed light on the case. For two centuries

University of California law students prepare to take an exam. Though it wasn't always this way, American lawyers are today highly trained.

American lawyers have based their arguments on previously decided cases. The ultimate legal decisions—or precedents—are those handed down by the highest court in the land: the U.S. Supreme Court. Not all matters reach the Supreme Court, however. Many important issues are resolved at lower court levels. Lawyers looking for case precedent can find material in different places.

This legal research once took the lawyer and staff an enormous amount of time (and contributed to high legal fees). In the old days researchers had to pore through law books and case records manually, page by page. During the latter decades of the 20th century, however, legal researchers began to rely increasingly on electronic tools. Voluminous archives of case decisions are stored on media that can be accessed by computers. Lawyers and their paralegals can now place a CD-ROM disk into a computer and, with a few typed commands, search whole volumes of laws and case decisions in seconds. By using an online legal research service like Westlaw or LexisNexis, the searcher can compare and organize cases and results in different ways.

The body of judicial decisions from American courts is enormous—and it's multiplying. Computers help lawyers keep up with the latest cases pertaining to their practice areas.

Computers also help them find valuable information related to their clients' cases. Using the Internet, they can find facts and sources concerning practically every imaginable topic, plus expert witnesses who might testify on their clients' behalf.

Meanwhile, computers give lawyers a handle on massive casebooks. Major trials may involve millions of documents and other exhibits, and many thousands of hours of deposition testimony. Computers can keep track of it all. When the lawyer needs a particular item out of the thousands or millions, the computer can find it with a quick word search.

If the tools of legal representation have multiplied,

so have the complexities of the law. Some skeptics hold that in many ways, the state of the American judicial system is little more commendable now than it was a century ago—and may even be worse.

What are some of the serious challenges and stigmas defense lawyers face? Here are three examples.

The Law as a Morass

A problem that increasingly confounds defense lawyers (and prosecutors) is that in our complex, changing world many legal questions are beyond the understanding of the typical jury. The terminology used by many expert witnesses is often over the heads of the jurors who must decide the issue. If jurors don't have a clear grasp of the subject being argued, how can they render an informed verdict? Even judges sometimes display ignorance in certain cases.

As we have seen, lawyers and their witnesses try to use essential storytelling skills to convey their viewpoint effectively to jurors. In high-tech, medical, scientific, abstract financial, and other types of cases that involve uncommon expertise, lawyers now visualize their ideas and exhibits for the jury's benefit wherever possible. Computer-generated graphics, animations, charts, and other kinds of sight-and-sound evidence are tremendous aids in simplifying difficult concepts. Still, many observers doubt that the average juror can satisfactorily digest the facts and arguments in certain cases.

Slow Justice

A long-controversial problem with the American system of justice is delay. Defenders today use the latest technology to research and prepare their cases quickly and in depth. Speedy process, however, is elusive.

Justice is delayed by the sheer number of cases on court dockets. The government has taken steps to relieve caseloads, funding more judgeships and staff positions throughout various court systems. However, skeptics believe this buildup of judicial services has not kept pace with rising caseloads.

The Lawyer as Culprit

Another long-standing problem for lawyers has been their image. They do not enjoy an especially popular reputation among the professions. And possibly no lawyers are more maligned than defense lawyers. Thanks to them, many Americans believe, robbers, rapists, murderers, swindlers, and drug lords go free, or go away laughing because their sentence was only a slap on the wrist. Million-dollar embezzlers escape with meaninglessly small fines. Defendants faced with multiple charges are likely to dodge justice on legal technicalities before their cases are even heard.

Critics believe that lawyers often use defendants' rights and judicial safeguards to shield the guilty. The insanity defense has become one of the critics' favorite targets, although statistics indicate that the defense is infrequently used and, when it is used, rarely successful.

Much of the recent controversy over the insanity defense stems from the case of John W. Hinckley Jr. On March 30, 1981, Hinckley tried to assassinate President Ronald Reagan outside a hotel in Washington, D.C. Firing six shots with a pistol, he wounded the president, press secretary James Brady, a Secret Service agent, and a policeman before Secret Service agents managed to subdue him. Television news teams captured the entire incident on videotape, which was played and replayed countless times on television throughout the nation. In the face of incontrovertible proof that Hinckley was the shooter, most people assumed that the case would be cut-and-dried.

Hinckley's attorney, Vincent Fuller, initially tried to work out a plea agreement. When prosecutors balked, Fuller mounted an insanity defense. At trial, he presented evidence that the young man was delusional; Hinckley's motive for the assassination attempt was to

As the TV cameras roll, Secret Service agents mob would-be assassin John Hinckley while other members of the presidential entourage check the wounded. When a jury found Hinckley not guilty by reason of insanity, many Americans were outraged —and public opinion of defense lawyers plummeted.

impress actress Jodie Foster. Ultimately the jury found Hinckley not guilty by reason of insanity.

Many Americans were outraged at the verdict, which seemed to fly in the face of common sense, and the public's image of the criminal justice system in general and defense lawyers in particular suffered a blow. The Hinckley trial also set off a heated debate regarding the validity of the insanity defense. Both the U.S. Senate and the House of Representatives held committee hearings on the issue. The attorney general warned that the "rights of criminals" had become more important than the "rights of society."

Whether they're innocent or guilty, whenever defendants in shocking criminal cases use such legal tactics as the insanity plea, the criminal justice system comes under renewed public scrutiny. And all lawyers have to weather a new round of blows to their professional image.

Abraham Lincoln wrote a century and a half ago: "There is a vague popular belief that lawyers are necessarily dishonest." "Popular belief" has decidedly worsened. Possibly no other professionals are the butt of more jokes and insults than lawyers.

The objective of criminal justice in a democracy, though, is fairness for both society and the defendant. "The concern that the American legal system has gone too far in protecting defendants is widespread and genuine," writes author Elaine Pascoe. "Yet so is the concern that innocent people will be railroaded into jail if law enforcement powers are unchecked."

Laws change with the generations. (In most states, leaving a horse untethered in front of a saloon is no longer considered a misdemeanor!) Changing times spawn changing crimes. Enforcement by the police becomes more complicated as new laws are enacted. Ensuring defendants' rights likewise becomes more challenging.

Dedicated professionals, young and old, are rising to meet the challenge. They understand that the role of the defense lawyer in our society is a noble one. It requires a special talent and passion, plus a determination to master the rules by which a complex society lives.

The rewards are enormous. In the words of lawyer-author Lisa Paddock: "Many of the great turning points in the nation's history have occurred in courtrooms."

Bibliography

Arbetman, Lee, and Richard L. Roe. *Great Trials in American History: Civil War to the Present.* St. Paul, Minn.: West Publishing Co., 1985.

Baker, Tamela. "The Way of the Just." *Jubilee* (Winter 2000).

Bennett, W. Lance, and Martha S. Feldman. *Reconstructing Reality in the Courtroom: Justice and Judgment in American Culture.* New Brunswick, N.J.: Rutgers University Press, 1981.

Blumberg, Abraham S. *Criminal Justice.* Chicago: Quadrangle Books, 1967.

_____. "The Practice of Law as Confidence Game: Organizational Cooptation of a Profession." Reprinted in *American Court Systems: Readings in Judicial Process and Behavior,* edited by Sheldon Goldman and Austin Sarat. San Francisco, W.H. Freeman and Company, 1978. First published in *Law and Society Review* 1 (1967).

Calabro, Marian. *Great Courtroom Lawyers.* New York: Facts on File, 1996.

Chadwick, Bruce. *Infamous Trials.* Philadelphia: Chelsea House, 1997.

Dershowitz, Alan M. *Reasonable Doubts: The O. J. Simpson Case and the Criminal Justice System.* New York: Simon & Schuster, 1996.

Friedman, Lawrence M. *Crime and Punishment in American History.* New York: BasicBooks, 1993.

Gustafson, Anita. *Guilty or Innocent?* New York: Holt, Rinehart and Winston, 1985.

Harmon, Daniel E. "Get with It—Graphics in Law Practice: A Necessity, Not an Option." *The Lawyer's PC,* June 1, 1997

_____. "Visual Impact: Techshow Keynoter Paints the Broad Picture." *The Lawyer's PC,* May 1, 1997.

Bibliography

Hewett, Joan. *Public Defender: Lawyer for the People*. New York: Lodestar Books, 1991.

Kerper, Hazel B. *Introduction to the Criminal Justice System*. 2nd ed. St. Paul, Minn.: West Publishing Co., 1979.

Knappman, Edward W., ed. *Great American Trials*. Detroit: Visible Ink Press, 1994.

Kolanda, Jo, and Patricia Curley. *Trial by Jury*. New York: Franklin Watts, 1988.

Mann, Kenneth. *Defending White-Collar Crime: A Portrait of Attorneys at Work*. New Haven, Conn.: Yale University Press, 1985.

Pascoe, Elaine. *America's Courts on Trial: Questioning Our Legal System*. Brookfield, Conn.: Millbrook Press, 1997.

Rice, Earle, Jr. *The O. J. Simpson Trial*. San Diego: Lucent Books, 1997.

Schrager, Sam. *The Trial Lawyer's Art*. Philadelphia: Temple University Press, 1999.

Index

Index

Index

DANIEL E. HARMON is associate editor of *Sandlapper: The Magazine of South Carolina* and editor of *The Lawyer's PC*, a national computer newsletter. He is the author of more than two dozen books, most of them nonfiction historical and humorous works and biographies. Harmon lives in Spartanburg, South Carolina.

AUSTIN SARAT is William Nelson Cromwell Professor of Jurisprudence and Political Science at Amherst College, where he also chairs the Department of Law, Jurisprudence and Social Thought. Professor Sarat is the author or editor of 23 books and numerous scholarly articles. Among his books are *Law's Violence, Sitting in Judgment: Sentencing the White Collar Criminal*, and *Justice and Injustice in Law and Legal Theory*. He has received many academic awards and held several prestigious fellowships. He is President of the Law & Society Association and Chair of the Working Group on Law, Culture and the Humanities. In addition, he is a nationally recognized teacher and educator whose teaching has been featured in the *New York Times*, on the *Today* show, and on National Public Radio's *Fresh Air*.

Picture Credits